Keeping Your Balance in an Immoral Age

Keeping Your Balance in an Immoral Age

Edited by
Sara L. Anderson

KEEPING YOUR BALANCE IN AN IMMORAL AGE
Copyright © 1988 by Forum for Scriptural Christianity, Inc.
Published by Bristol Books

First Printing, January 1988

All rights reserved. Except for brief quotations embodied in critical articles and reviews, no part of this book may be used or reproduced in any manner whatsoever without written permission.

Unless otherwise indicated, all Scripture quotations are from the *New American Standard Bible,* © 1960, 1963, 1968, 1971, 1972, 1973, 1975, 1977 by The Lockman Foundation. Used by permission.

Scripture quotations indicated Phillips are reprinted with permission of Macmillan Publishing Company from *The New Testament in Modern English,* revised edition by J.B. Phillips © J.B. Phillips 1958, 1960, 1972.

Library of Congress Card Number: 87-72706

ISBN:0-91785-06-4

Suggested Subject Headings:
1. Christian Ethics
2. Church and Social Problems

Recommended Dewey Decimal Classification: 241

BRISTOL BOOKS
An imprint of Good News, Forum for Scriptural Christianity, Inc.
308 East Main Street • Wilmore, Kentucky, 40390

Contents

1. Christian Taboos—Are They Valid Today? 7
2. How Television Affects Our Values 19
3. Can Homosexuality Be Healed? 29
4. Should the Christian Gamble? 39
5. Consequences of the Sexual Revolution 49
6. Obedience in the 'Little Things' 63
7. You *Can* Do Something About Pornography! 71
8. Dismissing Racial Misconceptions 81
9. The Church and Christians Who 'Live Together' 89
10. What Can *You* Do About Alcoholism? 99
11. Why Abortion Isn't the Answer 107
12. Divorce, Remarriage and the Bible 115
13. Morality Matters in Money Management 123

CHAPTER 1

Christian Taboos— Are They Valid Today?

One of my earliest encounters with a Christian taboo, one which has pretty much passed from the scene now, involved "mixed bathing." I didn't understand why it was "bathing" instead of "swimming." And since I was only six, the "mixed" part didn't mean much to me either.

What I did comprehend was this: It was summer in Georgiana, Alabama. Heat creased the air over the blacktop in front of my house and sucked the moisture out of my little body in streams. Tears ran together with sweat as I sat on the front porch—watching.

Across the street every kid in my first-grade class was splashing in the community swimming pool. On each face was a

---

R. Michael Sigler *is associate pastor of Gadsden Street United Methodist Church in Pensacola, Florida. He has a master's degree in communications from Wheaton College, Wheaton, Illinois.*

look of cool ecstasy. Or so it seemed to me. Paradise was a hop-and-a-dip away, but I was barred from entrance. We didn't believe in mixed bathing.

Years later, after that particular taboo had been repealed, my mother told me about her own childhood heartbreak over mixed bathing. Her parents hadn't believed in it either. But one day they let her go with some girlfriends down to an isolated creek bank to swim. The other girls wore swimsuits, but the taboo had an extra proviso in my mother's family — girls couldn't wear swimsuits, even when they "bathed" in unmixed company.

The thought of my mother jumping fully clothed, long dress flying, into that muddy creek has left an indelible impression on my mind's eye.

When I think about it, my sweltering porch across from the swimming pool seems almost tolerable.

We laugh about those episodes now, my mother and I, but never without a lingering stab of pain. Someone has said that most theology grows out of the theologian's personal experience. I'm no expert theologian, but living with the *do's and don'ts* of conservative Christianity has made me wonder a great deal about this matter of Christian taboos.

Since I have seen a number of them come and go—mostly go—within my lifetime, I'm left with questions. Are our taboos merely products of culture—irrelevant rules and regulations destined to change with the times? Is there a right way to determine Christian standards, particularly in the gray areas not specifically addressed by the Bible? What kinds of taboos should I impose on my children, and why?

Origins of Cultural Taboos

Many of our cultural taboos originated in an earlier era commonly associated with American fundamentalism. Fundamentalists and evangelicals share a common ancestry. And we have to look to the same historical sources to understand the origins of our taboos. To take such a look is to discover an awkward gap between past and present attitudes about things *worn, swallowed, projected on screens and sold on Sundays....*

At the Billy Graham Center in Wheaton, Illinois, you can take a walking tour of the history of American evangelism. I took it once, and one of the museum holdings I liked best was a little video box. You could switch it on yourself and view actual footage of the famous evangelist Billy Sunday.

It is a treat to watch. Sunday crouches down like a lion, then springs up, slams his fist into his empty hand and lunges toward the audience with his arm and forefinger aimed like a .44 magnum. All the while, in a hoarse voice, he's exhorting about some taboo or other: "I'll kick it as long as I've got a foot, and I'll fight it as long as I've got a fist. I'll butt it as long as I've got a head. I'll bite it as long as I've got a tooth. And when I'm old and fistless and footless and toothless, I'll gum it till I go home to glory and it goes home to perdition!"

In another sermon Sunday said, "The theater, as constructed today, is one of the rottenest institutions outside of hell...." "Card playing," declared Sunday, "is the most insidious contribution of vice in the world today."[1]

The theater was a favorite target of evangelist D.L. Moody, as well. He listed it as one of the "four great temptations that threaten us today."[2] Number three on his list was Sunday newspapers.

John Roach Straton was one of the best-known fundamentalists of his era. He pastored New York City's Calvary Baptist Church from 1918 to 1929. Straton believed the fashion industry had formed a secret conspiracy to change clothing styles as often as possible in order to keep the prices high.

His indignation boiled against the evils of worldly fashion: "Now we have a mixture of...styles, and every conceivable color of feather and flower has been pressed into service, until the sanctuary on Easter Sunday looks like a head-on collision between a flower garden and a poultry show." Straton had a solution to the problem too—a national costume which would be both modest and utilitarian, pretty but shorn of any sex appeal.[3]

An even less widely known fact is that Americans owe the invention of the ice cream sundae to some Christians' taboo. It seems that the saints in Evanston, Illinois, organized to prohibit the sale of ice cream sodas on the Lord's Day. They believed the fizz in the carbonated beverages would corrupt their young people. So the ice cream parlors dumped the soda part and began selling ice cream with a topping instead. The saints were satisfied, and the ice cream "sunday" was born.[4]

The list of bygone taboos is as long as a Pharisee's tassel: hairstyles, makeup, dress lengths (in the 1960s too much leg was the problem, in the 1920s too much *wrist* could give a girl a bad reputation), Sunday amusements, novels, movies, comic books, *ad infinitum.*

"But the problem today is that we don't have *any* standards!" someone is no doubt thinking. "The pendulum has swung too far the other way."

A prominent evangelical leader, a psychologist, recently remarked: "Ten or twelve years ago, most Christians I knew were so bound up and legalistic, I found myself talking to them almost exclusively about freedom in Christ. Today, just a decade or so later, evangelicals are so licentious and self-seeking, I find myself giving them boundaries from God's Word."[5]

Abandoning Traditional Taboos

Forget for a moment the part of the Church which doesn't even claim an allegiance to biblical norms. Look instead at today's evangelicals and our changing attitudes toward the gray areas of behavior and lifestyle. For good or ill, Bible-believing Christians are abandoning many of the traditional taboos faster than our grandparents could have said "it's of the devil."

Entertainment. Dress. The arts. Alcohol and tobacco. Attitudes about sex. In each of these areas, and many others, the gap between today's Christians and our forebears has widened.

There are many reasons for this gap. One observer claims that no less a pillar of conservative concerns than the late Francis

Schaeffer altered evangelical attitudes toward the arts.[6] Schaeffer encouraged young evangelicals to appreciate secular music, literature and art instead of rejecting all "worldly" culture as had the older evangelicals.

Evangelical hero C.S. Lewis may have done as much as any TV commercial to moderate evangelical attitudes toward smoking. To this Oxford don's many devotees, Lewis' pipe is an inextricable part of the way they remember him. That is not to say that, suddenly, Christians have declared smoking to be all right. But today's abstinence is based less on "spirituality" than on health.

In the area of human sexuality, evangelicals continue to hold to the biblical standard of chastity in singleness and fidelity in marriage. What is different today is the openness with which our teachers, preachers and authors discuss sex. When someone with the conservative credentials of Tim LaHaye can sell nearly a million copies of a book about sex for Christians (*The Act of Marriage*), the subject is far from being taboo.

Along with this new openness has come a reappraisal of some of the traditional prohibitions. For example, many of today's Christians apparently consider masturbation a normal and not necessarily sinful part of growing up. Best-selling pastor-author Charlie Shedd, for one, has called it "a gift of God."

"The Christian church," writes Dr. Karl Menninger in his book *Whatever Happened to Sin?*, "has generally taught the sinfulness of masturbation, although the Bible says virtually nothing about it....The amazing circumstance is that sometime after the turn of the present century, this ancient taboo, for the violation of which millions have been punished, threatened, condemned, intimidated and made hypocritical and cynical—a taboo thousands of years old—vanished almost overnight!"[7]

One may have reason to quarrel with Menninger's analysis or Shedd's endorsement, but that is not the point here. The point is that many evangelical Christians have quietly dropped yet another once-forbidden practice from their taboo lists.

Perhaps nowhere is the passing of a cultural taboo more obvious than in our attitudes toward the movies. Only 20 or 30 years ago many Christians would have shared the sentiments of the mother whose son informed her that he was going to see some missionary slides at church. She let him go, but not without a word of warning: "If those pictures start to move, you come on home!"

Now movie reviews are standard fare in evangelical magazines such as *Christianity Today* and *Eternity*. One December a few years ago *Eternity*, for example, included a review of the movie about Mozart, *Amadeus*. The reviewer enthusiastically recommended *Amadeus*, in spite of the fact that it includes "a desperate suicide attempt and vulgar gutter humor in quick juxtaposition." The review concludes, "*Amadeus* is bolder than most sermons.... See it for both spirit and soul."

Yes but....

There I was that very same December, on vacation, spending a night out with some old friends. We all grew up in the Bible belt, went to secular universities, struggled with our faith, but came out on the side of Christianity. One friend works for IBM. One is an ordained minister completing a doctoral thesis in church history. The other is a church music director.

We were seated around a table drinking coffee at the local steak place, trying to decide what movie to see. We'd narrowed the choices to four.

The first choice was nominated.

"Uh-uh. Terrible reviews."

"What's it about?"

"Adultery."

"Yeah, but it can't be too bad; it's rated PG."

"That just means they don't do it on the screen."

The second film was dismissed as too confusing.

Somebody lobbied for the biggest comedy hit of the season.

"Yeah, but it got an R rating. Every other word is spelled with four letters."

Help!

In the old days when the movies were taboo, about the worst thing a backslider might have seen was Rhett "damn"-ing Scarlett at the end of *Gone With the Wind*. Now that movie-going is generally accepted the trick is to find one that's not shot through with ilicit sex or a nauseating level of violence.

Did Taboos Fail?

But I wonder. What about all those taboos of an earlier era? Did they fail? And if they did, why?

In one sense, maybe it is *we* who have failed *them*.

The tidal wave of secularism keeps slamming against the Church, too often leaving serious cracks in our ethical foundations. We could use some of the moral backbone of a Moody or a Sunday today.

Still, in many ways, I do think the old taboo system failed. It failed partly because personal convictions formed out of a living relationship with Christ became dead, legalistic codes of behavior. The wine dried up, and all that was left was a stiff, cracking wineskin. Being Christian came to mean conforming to some group's external behavior code.

Another reason the old taboo system failed is because it substituted the traditions of men for the Word of God. It may be risky to stick to Biblical *principles*—a standard of "modesty," for example, rather than specific prescriptions for dress. But it is less risky than building a man-made taboo system.

The old taboo system failed also because it contributed to a kind of nearsightedness of the moral eye. When I was 12, church folks were all worked up about boys wearing their hair so long it touched their collars. That same year, Rev. Martin Luther King, Jr. led a freedom march from Selma to my hometown of Montgomery, Alabama. In their *more* charitable moments, those same church folks ignored the march.

Moral nearsightedness. We judge our spirituality by externals, and inside we're eaten up by pride and greed and prejudice. The "world" *is* too much with us—in the front row at church as well as the back row of the cinema.

I can't go back to the old taboo system for another reason: I know what it can do to *hurt* my witness.

I stumbled onto a young man toward the end of my weekly rounds as a one-day-a-week hospital chaplain. Gary, about 23, was facing surgery for a brain tumor and possible loss of his eyesight. He hadn't been to church for about seven years.

The good news about his conservative church background was that someone back there had told him, "If you ever want to get your life together with the Lord, try reading the Gospel of John." He was.

The bad news was that Gary's former church had placed a huge emphasis on its list of cultural taboos. The night before I visited him, on his own he had confessed his sin and placed his faith in Jesus Christ. "*Something* happened," he told me. "I've had so much joy ever since—and I'm not afraid."

But Gary wouldn't claim to be a Christian. He had a smoking habit he was trying to quit—he didn't think he could be accepted as a Christian till he had all the external taboos worked out.

Christian author Rosalind Rinker tells about a college freshman who was proud of herself for having witnessed to all the coeds in her dorm. "Now they all know where I stand in regard to worldly things," she informed Miss Rinker. The girl had told her dorm-mates that she didn't smoke, dance, play cards, go to movies or wear lipstick. "They all know I'm different and that I'm a Christian," she said heroically.

"Well, Jan," Miss Rinker replied with intended irony, "I suppose they all want to be like you now."[8] The girl's taboo system, rather than Jesus Christ, had become the focus of her witness to the world.

The old taboos failed, not because they were all wrong, but because they were based on a wrong emphasis.

Freed from Taboos?

But where does that leave me, an evangelical Christian

Christian Taboos—Are They Valid Today?   15

approaching the 21st Century, "freed" from the old taboo system? If evangelicals have been changing their minds about things like entertainment and dress, society at large has had a full-blown revolution in morals. And the bad news is, the other side has clearly won.

Now I must figure out what it means to be a Christian in a world where the bad guy is the one who *doesn't* accept extra-marital sex or the practice of homosexuality.

Is there a way forward? Or must we Christians isolate ourselves from the rest of society?

Perhaps we can yet find a way to move ahead. It might help to remember a few lessons from our experience with the old taboos.

Taboos may change in the gray areas (in the first century, eating idols' meat was high on the list). But some things *are* black and white. We don't need to rewrite the Ten Commandments. We must use the Bible as our guide. But let's be willing to part with the cultural trappings that have been added to it.

We must learn to apply the Apostle Paul's teaching about taboos. It can be stated like this: Gray areas thou wilt always have with you. Every Christian won't come out at the same place on these matters—don't fight over them or judge each other. Let each brother follow his conscience. You have liberty to decide for yourself, but don't forget that your actions affect others too (1 Corinthians 8).

This leads to that old taboo bugaboo, "the weaker brother." Paul cautioned against letting our freedom cause others to stumble. But don't forget, he never intended that this argument be dragged out every time the more completely uncompromising group needs a club to control those who are more flexible.

When he coined the term, Paul was talking about new, baby Christians who were too immature to let go of some morally-neutral cultural taboos. But the people we call weaker brothers today are usually older Christians determined to make everybody else fit their particular taboo system.

Finally, I suspect that to find our way forward on the taboo question, without slipping into legalism or license, we will have to take a fresh look at *holiness*. No matter that the word is too often associated with bunned hair and rigid behavior codes. No matter that its mention in some circles is a theological *faux pas*.

Whatever holiness means or does not mean, it must have something to do with operating ethically *from the inside out*. "Holy people do what God says, but doing what God says does not make them holy."[9]

Holiness, in its basic meaning of "setapartness" to God, may yet be the answer. But only as we drop the excess cultural baggage and let God write His laws on our hearts. Only when we realize it's *us* he wants, not our money, our talents or our conforming to a man-made taboo system.

Notes

1. Theodore Frankenberg, *The Spectacular Career of Rev. Billy Sunday*.
2. D.L. Moody, *Moody's Latest Sermons*, pp.52-60.
3. John R. Straton, Menace of Immorality, p. 12.
4. Matilda Nordvedt, "Old-Fashioned Laws and New-Styled Freedom," Fundamentalist Journal, Nov.1984, pp. 28-29.
5. Quoted in Peter E. Gillquist's *Why We Haven't Changed the World*, p. 36.
6. Richard Quebedeaux, *The Worldly Evangelicals*, p. 117.
7. Karl Menninger, MD., *Whatever Became of Sin?*, p. 36.
8. Rosalind Rinker, *You Can Witness with Confidence*, p. 24.
9. Gillquist, p. 137.

Discussion Questions

1. Think of one taboo you abided by in childhood that no longer seems to be an issue with most Christians today? Why do you think it is no longer an issue?

2. Think of a taboo you still hold to. Why is it important to you? Is your reasoning grounded in scripture or tradition?

3. Why do you think the old taboo system broke down?

4. Why does it seem harder to stick to "principles" rather than specific "rules" of behavior?

5. In what ways has the taboo system contributed to "moral nearsightedness" (page 13)?

6. Why do we seem to elevate some sins, considering them worse in God's eyes (i.e., going to R-rated movies vs. gossiping about fellow church members)?

7. In what ways can living by a rigid set of rules hurt our witness to the world (page 13)?

8. How then can we live by high moral standards without damaging our witness to the world?

9. In what instances should the principle of "the weaker brother" be invoked (page 15)? When should it not be used to respond to someone else's freedom?

CHAPTER 2

How Television Affects Our Values

Picture this true story.

A minister and his family were attending an inspirational conference. Its aim was to find ways of promoting the teaching of biblical principles in the church.

The conference discussions were exhilarating and inspiring, but mentally taxing. So when the family members got back to their hotel room, they agreed to relax with some television.

"Dallas" was on. Dad, Mom and the kids watched enthralled as J.R. Ewing plotted the destruction of his brother Bobby. J.R.'s wife, Sue Ellen, conducted her latest affair. A formerly loving couple met awkwardly at a party. And J.R. was trying to cover up a murder. The minister's family took it all in, oblivious to the irony of the situation.

James S. Robb *is Executive Editor of* Good News *magazine and Editor-in-Chief of Bristol Books in Wilmore, Kentucky.*

Welcome to the world of Christian schizophrenia. People who have pledged to turn the other cheek enjoy watching vice cops, vigilantes and drug dealers turn people's cheeks into blood and bruises. It's a world where church members committed to moral purity soak up plots revolving around unmarried couples who routinely spend the night together. (Only the AIDS scare has caused script writers to turn down the heat a little.)

Christians of all theological stripes have taken stands on scores of social and moral questions. Somewhere on everyone's list of moral problems has been the terrible state of television programming.

But for most Christians the problems of television have been overshadowed by the issues of alcohol abuse, hunger, abortion and school prayer. In fact, many Christians have become accustomed to uncritically using TV to escape the pressures of daily life.

However, a new batch of evidence is piling up which suggests the Christian community may be far too apathetic about television; that television may be one of the most destructive forces in America today; that TV is getting worse all the time. In short, growing evidence suggests that TV should move up higher on the priority list of Christian moral concerns.

Experts point out several types of damaging elements including violence, sex, profanity, anti-social actions and swipes at the Christian faith.

Promiscuity as the Norm

By far the most common charge against television is that it portrays unhealthy levels of illicit sexual material and a value system that accepts promiscuity as the norm. Of course networks respond by claiming they don't exploit sex and that everything they do is in good taste. But those who monitor television programming draw other conclusions.

A recent report on TV sex, violence and profanity published by the National Federation for Decency gives a sordid picture of TV shows saturated by sexual content. The NFD, headed by United Methodist minister and activist Donald Wildmon, had volunteer monitors watching every prime-time network show for 12 consecutive weeks in the fall of 1986. The report attests to 2,353 sexually-related incidents on evening network shows during those three months.

Of course no one person can watch all three networks simultaneously. But if a child watched the three hours of prime-time programming by a single network, CBS for example, each day of the three months of the report, he or she would have seen suggested sexual intercourse by unmarried people a total of 203 times.

That's more than twice an evening. Compare that to the one hour a week in Sunday school where children are taught values like fidelity in marriage. If parents do not take the time to reinforce these values, it's a small wonder children adopt the philosophies of television characters.

The NFD report reveals that sexually suggestive comments were made by TV characters almost twice each hour. Even more interesting is the comparison of sexually related incidents between couples who were married and couples who were not. The report states that allusions to sex between unmarried couples occurred five and one-half times as often as sex involving married couples.

Even advertisements for upcoming shows play up the sexual aspects of the program. One ABC ad for back-to-back shows contained these "teasers":

> To prove she's not jealous, a single woman tells her male downstairs neighbor, "You're entitled to have sex with anyone you want." That is followed by a middle-aged man asking a co-worker, "How would you feel about having non-stop, unbridled sex tonight? I'll spring for dinner."

Sexual content is common on both regular series programming and made-for-TV movies. Feature-length motion pictures run on the public air waves can be even more explicit. Commercial stations frequently air R-rated movies which, even in a censored form, contain a warning that the subject matter may be objectionable to some viewers or inappropriate for children.

Add to that the subtle messages many television writers use to push their private agendas, messages like "Abortion is a reasonable way to deal with an unwanted pregnancy," or "A homosexual lifestyle is perfectly normal, and those (like evangelical Christians) who disagree with this perspective are narrow-minded, prudish bigots."

The second most common charge against TV is that it makes violence trivial, commonplace and even amusing. The NFD report states that the three networks depicted 2,105 acts of violence on evening shows during the three months of monitoring. That's an average of three violent acts an hour per network.

Studies also indicate television's preoccupation with profanity. The NFD says that programs average about five incidents of profanity per hour per network. It wasn't that long ago when "darn" was about the crudest word on broadcast TV. Today neither irritated cops nor criminals hesitate to refer to one another as a "son-of-a-bitch." In a popular mystery-comedy, the hero and heroine referred to each other as "bitch" and "bastard" before heading off to the bedroom.

Anti-social and Anti-faith

Anti-social behavior is another consideration. TV characters are impolite, abusive, lacking in self-control, overly aggressive and generally incorrigible. A study published by the *Phi Delta Kappan* magazine examined this element. The author of the study first discovered the TV shows most popular with young children in one particular area of the country.

The researcher then asked his monitors to see how often a positive social action, such as politeness, was depicted on the shows versus the number of times negative values were displayed. He found positive and negative values were shown nearly the same number of times. But when he tabulated the *intensity* of the actions, he discovered the negative social values were given double the intensity as the positive ones. In other words, a TV character might mumble a polite thank-you to his mother just before beating an enemy into senseless submission.

And how about that last category—slurs against the Christian faith? It happens more frequently than we care to admit.

A study done for *Public Opinion* magazine on media decision makers indicated that media brass do not generally attend religious services. An overwhelming 86 percent seldom or never go to church or synagogue. Considering that nearly half of all Americans attend services at least once a week, shapers of the media are by contrast strikingly unreligious.

This lack of faith is evident on the TV screen. Often ministers are portrayed as weak, fearful and lacking in character, or they are hell-fire and brimstone preachers. Christian lay people are frequently presented as rigid, dogmatic kill-joys—especially for their idea that sex should be confined to monogamous marriage.

The frightening thing about all this is that trends point to a further dropping in the moral content of television. With a few noteworthy exceptions, many shows are raising the levels of violence and/or sex.

Cable networks like Home Box Office and Showtime are raising the stakes considerably in terms of sordid behavior. Increasing numbers of households are now paying a monthly fee to bring uncut R-rated movies into their homes. Network shows begin to look tame next to the explicit gore and sexual behavior exhibited during cable programming. HBO and other services usually reserve their most explicit films for late evening viewing, but children old enough to read are old enough to turn the dial to those movies when their parents aren't around.

Once Christians learn just how destructive much of television programming has become they generally disapprove. But is TV content a mere nuisance? Can television become a danger to families who view it?

Dr. Thomas Radecki, founder of the National Coalition on TV Violence cites a great deal of evidence indicating that kids and adults who watch violent TV shows commit violent acts themselves. And U.S. Surgeon General C. Everett Koop, an evangelical Christian and a vocal opponent of television violence, issued a report linking TV violence to real violence.

Radecki sees the same connection. He says, "It's a very common finding of mine that families having a high level of anger...will also have a high level of violent entertainment." He contends that violence is so disturbing because it encourages the emotion of anger in people viewing it. "Anger is only one of many ways that people can respond to frustration," he says.

The relationship of television sex to the moral decisions of real persons is a little more slippery. It is true that the moral content of TV has been declining at the same time traditional sexual mores have been breaking down in our society. But defenders of television argue that TV is just following society, not leading it.

Protection from Programming

There might be some truth in that for adult viewers. But the problem with network TV is that programs are not given ratings of G, PG and R as are the movies. Every show is piped into every home, and mom and dad aren't always there to turn off offensive programming. How immune can children be to TV's depiction of abusive and promiscuous sex?

Recent data concerning teenage viewing is especially frightening: The average teenager now watches between 24 and 25 hours of TV each week. That's nearly the same number of hours he or she spends in school (figured on a year-round average).

When sex and violence are featured in a single program, the results can be easily measured. Radecki's organization caught sight of a press report about a 12-year-old boy who had lured a little girl to his parents' basement and sexually molested her near a pool table. The boy's parents told police the boy had been watching the 1984 televised trial of the Massachusetts men accused of raping a young woman on a barroom table. Similar reports are becoming more common.

Daytime television is not studied as frequently, but consider the number of people, including Christians, who hate to miss afternoon dramas. Many folks, women *and* men take their lunch hours to catch up on the latest illegitimate pregnancy, extramarital affair, abortion, drug deal, murder or case of amnesia on their favorite soap.

The only effective way to help protect yourself and your family from the potentially damaging effects of TV is to turn it off or to become extremely selective in choosing which programs your family watches. But being selective is tough. Even children's cartoons like "G.I. Joe" and "The Transformers" can be extremely violent. And "quality" shows like "L.A. Law" and "Cagney and Lacey" are often filled with sexual material and anti-social behavior.

Christians do have more options where cable TV service is available. The Christian Broadcasting Network and other such systems offer programs decidedly more wholesome than the networks' fare, although CBN has rightly been accused of broadcasting programs too violent for some people's taste.

With videotape recorders now in common use, many parents choose to tape a possibly questionable television program and preview it before deciding whether to let the kids watch it later.

Of course, it's easier to turn off your own set than to convince the networks to alter their programming. But several groups are trying anyway, believing citizens have a responsibility to improve TV.

The NFD, CLeaR-TV (Christian Leaders for Responsible TV, an ecumenical group) and the National Coalition on TV Violence discourage people from writing the networks, since executives tend to ignore everything but the ratings and the advertisers. Instead, they say, concerned individuals should note programs they find offensive and write the sponsors. Letters should be polite but should bluntly threaten to stop buying a sponsor's products if it keeps sponsoring offensive shows.

The record clearly proves that organized boycotts and pressure campaigns against TV advertisers can help bring reform to the tube. When an organization called the Coalition for Better Television was threatening to boycott sponsors a few years ago, the chairman of TV's biggest advertiser, Proctor and Gamble, announced he partly agreed with the Coalition. "We think the coalition is expressing some very important and broadly-held views about gratuitous sex, violence and profanity." The chairman's remarks frightened the networks into temporarily airing a better class of programming. More recently, CLeaR-TV, has achieved success by boycotting and threatening to boycott sponsors of programming they deem objectionable.

NFD leaders believe the most important thing a Christian can do is talk to his or her pastor and convince him or her of the urgency of this problem. Only when churches organize and decide to boycott and/or write letters to sponsors, will TV be cleaned up.

Discussion Questions

1. Think about your favorite television program. List the programs you watch regularly. Do they reinforce what you consider to be Christ-like values? Why? Why not?

2. Read Philippians 4:8. Consider the content of the programs as compared to Paul's list of things to think about. What is your reaction?

3. Do you schedule your evening or week around a favorite program? Do you rush out of church to get home in time for the afternoon football game?

4. In what ways do you think television affects your values? Does something that would have offended you five years ago now seem a normal occurrence?

5. Evaluate the amount of time your family spends watching television— and what you watch. Should you change your TV routine at all? How?

6. Even if you do not watch television, does it affect you indirectly? If so, how?

7. If you are a parent, sit down and watch your children's favorite TV program with them. Do you agree with the values presented in the program? Discuss with them why the values are good or bad.

CHAPTER 3

Can Homosexuality Be Healed?

Andy Comisky remembers being different from the other little boys in his neighborhood. His childhood recollections include an early gravitation to "feminine" things. Another memory is of becoming increasingly sensitive to remarks about his masculinity, or lack of it. The onset of puberty brought with it the realization that his sexual desires were geared toward males.

Instead of seeking counseling to gain perspective on his sexual confusion, Andy began to entertain the idea of embracing the gay lifestyle after finishing high school. He was reading the secular literature about homosexuality; it was telling him that being gay was OK, that in fact it would be healthy for him to explore his sexual orientation toward males.

Rick Grant *is a freelance television writer. He is a member of Vineyard Christian Fellowship in Santa Monica, California.*

So he did. But after becoming involved in the gay lifestyle Andy began to re-evaluate his "liberating" move. He realized accepting the view that he was "born" homosexual had done nothing to relieve his inner struggle for self-identity.

That realization led ultimately to a new discovery—the healing power of Jesus Christ. After giving his life to Christ at a concert and "vowing through my ignorance to live for Jesus," Andy slowly but surely came to see himself as a new creature in Christ. Although "the tension between the flesh and the Spirit seemed almost unbearable at times," he chose to accept the strength and grace God provided.

Andy and his wife, Annette, parents of three children, operate a ministry in Santa Monica, California that helps others who struggle with homosexuality. The organization, which ministers to an average of 300 individuals a week, is one of a number of ex-gay ministries throughout the country. They offer counseling and spiritual nurture to homosexually-oriented persons who desire to be healed.

The significant number of men and women who seek and receive healing from homosexuality shows that Andy's story is not an isolated experience. For many homosexuals, God's love and forgiveness breaks through the tangled web of identity confusion and sinful behavior.

In her book, *The Healing of the Homosexual*, psychologist Leanne Payne writes: "As a sexual neurosis, homosexuality is regarded as one of the most complex. As a condition for God to heal, it is (in spite of the widespread belief to the contrary) remarkably simple."

But isn't a person's sexual orientation involuntary? Don't homosexuals need acceptance rather than attempts to help them change?

While the complexities of the issue can't be denied, the growing consensus among persons who minister to homosexuals is that gay persons need not be permanently bound to their sexual lifestyle or orientation. Unfortunately, many Christians make the same mistake Andy Comisky made. They've bought into the prevailing societal wisdom which views homosexuality as unalterable.

Individual Christians are not totally to blame for the lack of insight concerning homosexuality. The Church has historically propagated imbalanced viewpoints, ranging from a denial of homosexuality's existence to full-scale acceptance. For many years the Church kept the subject of homosexuality in the closet. The Church simply was not there when the homosexual struggler needed guidelines, fellowship and care.

But in recent years the prompting of God's Word, coupled with increasingly accurate statistics concerning the prevalence of homosexuality (5-10 percent of both the Christian and non-Christian populations are reported to be affected), has caused the Church to examine its head-in-the-sand approach. The Bible teaches that "all have sinned" and that God doesn't use a sin rating system. As a result Christians have seen their need to forsake judgmental attitudes.

In some circles, however, the loving arms of acceptance have embraced the *practice* of homosexuality along with the practitioners. Gay and lesbian churches now claim more than 50,000 members across the nation. The leaders of these congregations endorse the gay lifestyle and entreat their congregations to "come out of the closet."

Is Homosexuality Sinful?

Two pivotal questions arise when dealing with any discussion of homosexuality and Christianity. The first question concerns whether or not homosexuality is sinful. The second deals with the genetic or innate aspects of homosexuality—that is, are people born homosexual?

The teaching of the Bible consistently opposes the homosexual lifestyle. In both the Old and New Testaments sex is affirmed within the context of a committed heterosexual union (wholeness in two halves). But scripture condemns homosexual practices, as in Paul's description of "men with men committing indecent acts and receiving in their own persons the due penalty of their error" (Romans 1:27).

It is important to emphasize that the overt *act* of homosexuality is sinful, not the *temptation* toward homosexuality. A person may have a predisposition toward homosexuality (or may just be experiencing an occasional misguided emotion or bizarre dream), but he or she is held accountable when the temptation leads to a sexual encounter.

With this in mind it is vitally important that a person who struggles with homosexual feelings seeks counseling before getting involved in homosexual activity. People with faulty perceptions of their homosexual urges often begin to internalize the gay identification. And they may consign themselves to what they feel is an inevitable lifestyle.

One former lesbian told of breaking up with her boyfriend of two years and then having homosexual dreams. Not realizing that such dreams are not uncommon among heterosexual people from time to time, she went to a psychologist who encouraged her to investigate her feelings. After finding an unhappy version of the "gay life" on Sunset Strip in Hollywood, she gave her life to Christ. That was the beginning of her healing process.

A more difficult question to answer than whether or not homosexuality is sinful concerns the validity of a genetic or hormonal predisposition toward homosexuality. This debate centers on whether sexual preference is determined biologically or is learned behavior.

Those who favor a biological predisposition emphasize that hormonal or chromosomal differences in individuals lead to a tendency toward either heterosexuality or homosexuality. Because this tendency exists, it is argued, homosexuality should be viewed as normal. Although some studies have suggested that homosexual men have lower androgen (male hormone) levels than heterosexual men, the evidence has not been conclusive.

Those who support the environmental position believe that the child's sexual preference is not predetermined but learned.

Although the debate continues, there is increasing evidence that supports the learned-preference position.

In a study by E. Mansell Pattison and Myrna Loy Pattison entitled "'Ex-Gays': Religiously Mediated Change in Homosexuals" (*American Journal of Psychiatry*, December, 1980), an evaluation was made of 11 men who claimed to have changed sexual orientation from exclusive homosexuality to exclusive heterosexuality through participation in fellowship groups in a Pentacostal church.

The Pattisons concluded their report by saying: "Finally, the data suggests the importance of our concepts of homosexuality. When homosexuality is defined as an immutable and fixed condition that must be accepted, the potential for change seems slim. In our study, however, when homosexuality was defined as a changeable condition it appears that change was possible."

If homosexuality is learned (as the evidence suggests), then it can be unlearned. If it is a sin, then it can be forgiven. Gays no longer need to view themselves as having a fixed, permanent condition.

But merely stating that environmental factors are the most important cause does not mean that analyzing them is an easy task. There is no simple cause-and-effect relationship between any one given factor and a person's predisposition toward homosexuality.

There are a variety of reasons why someone enters homosexuality. Sometimes a child enters into it as a result of being abused or by misunderstanding male/female role models. Leanne Payne calls this role model confusion an identity crisis. "Homosexuals are often separated from some valid part of themselves through their failure to be affirmed as children," she says. "This separation, which stems from a symbolic confusion in the mind, usually shows up in their emotions."

Pattern of Healing

No matter what sexual predisposition a person might have, or why, the ex-gay ministries have demonstrated that Christ's power can heal sexual confusion. The healing process may be long and difficult, but it *can* happen—if the individual seeks the forgiveness and restoration Christ offers.

Leaders of ex-gay ministries point to a common pattern of healing which is often (but not always) present. Christians who wish to help homosexuals should have a good working knowledge of this pattern.

The first stage in the healing process is often a *turning-point event*, which causes the person to reevaluate his or her homosexual lifestyle. The nature of the "event" may vary greatly (i.e., a young man watches his lover die of AIDS, a woman finds her mate unfaithful), but this turning point has the effect of causing the person to pause and reflect.

The next stage in the healing process is the *acceptance of Christ as Savior*. In some cases this precedes the turning-point event. In other cases, becoming a Christian is the turning point. Whatever the chronological order, the important consideration is that the person gives his or her life to the Lord to begin the redemptive process.

In accepting God's forgiveness through Christ, the homosexual can in turn forgive God (releasing Him for damaging past events over which the person had no control), forgive others (giving up harsh feelings or desires to get even) and forgive himself or herself (a release from the condemnation of past sins and/or failure to live up to personal expectations).

During the *break away* period the person may desire to "get away from it all" by isolating himself or herself from gay friends, gay establishments and gay social groups. This breakaway often leads the individual to experience mood swings, loneliness and a sense of separation.

The need for disclosure becomes paramount at this stage. More than any factor, ex-gays point to a close friend as the most important aspect in the change process. Just "being there" for the ex-gay person, while letting him dictate the degree of self-disclosure, is often enough to give the recovering homosexual confidence to move ahead with his or her new identity.

The *new identity* stage includes an increasing dissatisfaction with the label "homosexual." At first the term "former homosexual" or "ex-gay" ("and such *were* some of you," 1 Corinthians 6:11) is helpful. Later the person will often want to make a complete break by casting off the homosexual label altogether.

As old hurts become resolved the fears of relating to the opposite sex may begin to disappear. The ex-gay person may begin to establish close relationships with the opposite sex or begin to contemplate marriage in a positive way. But although the desire to marry can be a positive step in the healing process, it should not be considered as the proof of change.

Support from the Church

Besides understanding these patterns (which, it should be noted, are not a pat formula for homosexual healing), the relative or friend who wants to be of help should try to steer the gay person into establishing a relationship with a church. Without accountability to a community of believers, he or she is more likely to drift back into the old lifestyle.

Comisky sees the church's job as "establishing a nurturing environment which not only upholds the truth but also gives a framework for change. The church shouldn't have a 'do-it-now-or-else' attitude but should give the homosexual space to repent."

The redemptive process can also be seen as a joint effort between the loved ones and the church. Group or individual intercession is of vital importance. Relatives and friends need to stand with the homosexual who is trying to change and love him or her through the experience.

Churches can help homosexuals through support groups, pastoral counseling and by helping to integrate the person into established Bible studies or kinship groups. Support groups might include discussion and Bible study times for those struggling with homosexuality, or groups might be formed to help spouses, relatives and friends air their feelings and seek guidance.

Homosexuals desperately need an informed and loving Church to tell them the truth about their identity in Christ. If the Church doesn't fill this role, the secular world is ready and willing to suggest "liberated" alternatives.

Discussion Questions

1. For much of its history, the Church has chosen not to openly discuss the problems of homosexual tendencies and homosexual practice. Why do you think this is so?

2. Why is it especially important that the Church address the issue now?

3. How would you answer the question, "Is homosexuality really a sin?"

4. A homosexual couple moves into the apartment next to yours. Some of the neighbors find out about their sexual orientation and leave them threatening messages. How can you, as a Christian, indicate that God cares for them even though their lifestyle is not pleasing to Him.

5. Respond to the comment: "I can't help my sexual orientation. God made me this way—I should celebrate His creation."

6. How would you respond if your son announced that he was gay? If a woman in your congregation confessed to being a lesbian and asked for prayer?

CHAPTER 4

Should the Christian Gamble?

Several years ago Anwar Wazzen was down on his luck. The Syrian-born man had come to the casinos in Atlantic City, New Jersey, to try to regain his fortune after his business partner in the Middle East had bilked him out of his share of their chocolate factory.

But instead of winning his fortune back, Wazzen's luck spiraled downward. Obsessed by the idea of becoming a millionaire again, he lost thousands at the gaming tables. As he continued to gamble, the more he lost. The more he lost, the more obsessed he became with the prospect of winning. Finally he'd lost everything. He couldn't even afford a plane ticket home.

William Alnor, *an award-winning investigative reporter from Darby, Pennsylvania, is the editor of the "National and International Religion Report" published in Roanoke, Virginia.*

The Atlantic City police found Wazzen at the top of a bridge attempting to muster enough courage to fling himself into an icy inlet. Fortunately for Wazzen, the Atlantic City Rescue Mission took him in, and after his conversion to Christianity he began to rebuild his life. Today Wazzen is the cook for the Rescue Mission.

Unfortunately for many other compulsive gamblers, things don't work out as well. During the winter, Atlantic City emergency officials occasionally find the frozen bodies of gamblers who have lost all they own. And the Rescue Mission and other shelters are always crammed with people who have fallen victim to the city's casinos. The number of people being treated for compulsive gambling at various institutions is swelling daily.

Yet despite the negative effect gambling has had on Atlantic City since the first casino opened in 1977, there are annual drives throughout America to try to bring gambling into more and more cities. Some analysts believe that the big money being spent to promote gambling, often by the wealthy casino industry, will entice more cities and resort areas to allow the opening of casinos.

This shouldn't be surprising. Americans largely accept some forms of gambling already. Even churches advertise "Bingo nights." Horse and dog racing is accepted in many states. Most striking, though, is the number of governments that sanction gambling in the form of lotteries. Contest fever has never been higher. People work very hard daily thinking up numbers, following racing news, filling out entry forms and spending money on a chance—one in billions at times—to be able to quit their jobs forever.

Cornell University professor G. Robert Blakey has noted the alarmingly high cost of lotteries. After studying state lotteries for two years for the Law Enforcement Assistance Administration he came to a blunt conclusion: "No one but a fool would gamble with state run (lotteries)."

They are "inefficient, inappropriate functions of state government, they create more gamblers by whetting the appetite, they have the potential for abuse, they simply postpone the day of reckoning for states that see them as new sources of wealth, and they are mere illusions of new revenues," he concluded.

The current lottery systems and the getting-something-for-nothing mentality are one of many forces helping to shred the fabric of society.

The Lottery Explosion

Lottery fever began in the early 1960s, when many states began seeking new ways to raise revenue without raising taxes. Also coming into play was the increasing liberalization of society's moral values and the growing muscle and financial power of gambling interests. One by one the states began to see lotteries as means to acquire new revenue.

So lotteries became popular in many states. They were walking a road this country had traveled in the past. Americans had already unsuccessfully experimented with lotteries. In 1777 the Continental Congress sponsored a lottery to help pay for the war against the British, and three New England states contributed with their own lotteries to help with the war effort. The trend continued through most of the 19th century. All states had banned them by the 1890s because of the widespread corruption and swindling that accompanied them.

Today, less than 20 years after the advent of state-sponsored lotteries, scholars, and community and church leaders are increasingly re-learning the lessons of our forefathers. Lotteries have not become a force to build society's projects; instead they are a force that erodes society. Scholars are also finding that lotteries don't eliminate the illegal numbers games (often linked to organized crime). They seem to have the opposite effect. And instead of pulling a financial burden off governments' backs, lotteries add to it.

The Commission on Review of the National Policy toward Gambling reported in 1976 that "participation in illegal gambling is greater in states where legal gambling is available than in states where no form of gambling exists."

Connecticut started a lottery to cut into illegal gambling and organized crime. But Austin J. McGuigan, the state's chief attorney, observed, "Rather than cut into the revenue of organized crime, the state has been swept by a gambling mania, which has more than doubled the level of illegal wagering in the last eight years."

In a study of Atlantic City gambling operations, authors George Sternlieb and James W. Hughes concurred: "Gambling of any kind encourages more gambling. Far from feeling the sting of competition, illegal operations find more clients."

Compulsive Gamblers

Another reason lotteries are not worth it is that they make poor business sense. Nationally, lotteries provided only an average of 2.8 percent of the revenues for the 17 states that ran them in 1983.

Only 40 percent of the revenue from a state lottery goes into something other than the lottery. The other 60 percent pays for prizes, administration and expensive advertising campaigns. In larger states such as New York and Pennsylvania, promoting the lotteries costs millions per year. And often the promotional campaigns target those who can least afford to play the lottery—poor people who are desperate to improve their condition in life.

When interest in the Illinois lottery dropped some years ago, an agency was commissioned to determine who played the games. The study indicated that prime markets for lottery sales were the disadvantaged neighborhoods of low income blacks and Hispanics.

Following the study the state launched a $9 million-a-year ad campaign which included placing billboards in ghetto areas of Chicago trumpeting: "How to Get from Washington Boulevard to Easy Street."

Church leaders working in the inner city have long been concerned over how lotteries exploit the poor by playing upon their plight. Rev. Thomas O'Gorman, of St. Malachy's Parish in Chicago, was angered over the amount of money wasted on the lottery and asked his parish of low-income families to bring in their losing lottery tickets. One Sunday more than 300 families brought in $5,000 worth of losing tickets.

In California a local television program focusing on lottery losers interviewed a man who had wall-papered a room of his house with losing tickets.

Another reason lotteries should be rejected is that they become a step on the way for individuals to become compulsive gamblers. Often called the "addiction of the 80s," compulsive gambling has become one of the fastest growing problems in America. According to Arnold Wexler, executive director of the Council on Compulsive Gambling of New Jersey, there are more than 400,000 active compulsive gamblers in New Jersey, affecting 350,000 spouses and 700,000 children. Thirty percent of all compulsive gamblers also have another addiction such as alcoholism or drug dependency. The attempted suicide rate of the compulsive gambler is 20 times higher than the national average and the spouse's attempted suicide rate is 15 times higher than the national average.

Wexler, a recovered compulsive gambler, also provided these statistics:

— 68 percent of the women used illegal means to finance their gambling (bad checks and employee theft were the most common crimes).

— Surveys of male and female prisoners in New Jersey, Michigan and Washington D. C. found that 30 to 40 percent were probably pathological gamblers.

— 13 percent of the prisoners acknowledged that they were in prison because of gambling-related problems.

— 96 percent of all compulsive gamblers started gambling before age 14. In Atlantic City alone from July 1, 1985 through June 30, 1986, 171,291 juveniles were prevented from entering a casino and 35,152 were escorted from a casino.

Another hidden cost of legalized gambling is the crime associated with it. The American Insurance Institute has estimated that as many as 40 percent of white collar crimes, such as embezzlement, can be traced to compulsive gambling.

If one thinks lotteries cause damage to the social fabric, the situation is far worse when casino gambling moves into an area. Take Atlantic City, New Jersey, for example, which won the right to have casino gambling in 1974 following a lavish promotion in which its sponsors convinced the voters that the casinos would rebuild decaying Atlantic City and that organized crime would be kept out.

But casino gambling has not been Atlantic City's savior. Many of the city's elderly and black populations have been pushed out by rising rent and real estate costs. The city has not been rebuilt—the casinos used loopholes to avoid reinvesting in the city. And remaining land was largely purchased by the casinos after a rash of mysterious arson fires razed dilapidated buildings in the city.

Crime has also increased at an alarming pace, climbing in direct proportion with the rising casino industry in the city. Atlantic City now boasts a massive police force to combat the high murder and violent crime rate—that's in addition to the private security forces the casinos employ.

Christians and Gambling

The growing concern about gambling is not new. For centuries many Christians have believed it to be wrong. In A.D. 306, for example, the Ecclesiastical Council of Elvira prescribed a year of public penance for any Catholic involved in a game of chance.

Today in America many Christians citing biblical reasons still believe gambling to be wrong. The first has to do with being a "good steward" of our time and of our money.

In the Parable of the Talents (Matthew 25) Jesus rebuked the man with the one talent because he hid the talent in the ground instead of investing it and gaining more talents to give to the master, as did the men who were given five and two talents.

Although there is some debate over what "talents" are and whether they refer to spiritual matters, few can argue over the poor business and time management judgments of gambling. (For example, Atlantic City gaming officials put player losses at more than $2.2 billion in 1985, up $250 million from 1984 figures.)

But more basic to many Christians is the philosophy of gambling. Why do people gamble? Why do they play the lotteries throughout many states today? Some do it for the excitement. But studies have shown that a prime motivation is the hope of gaining enough money to be comfortable for life without having to work. Is it biblical to hope to get through life without working? Many think not. God ordered Adam to work for a living after the Fall in the garden (Genesis 3). And Paul told the Thessalonians that he in the community who doesn't work, shouldn't eat (2 Thess. 3:10).

Christians also ought to know better than to believe that wealth will bring happiness. But many winners have become disenchanted. In California, for example, people found to be illegal aliens have been deported following the notoriety of a big win. Others have had to turn over their winnings to cover back taxes or delinquent child support. Still others complain of being approached by every charity imaginable and of the pressure applied by friends and relatives wanting to borrow money. One winner of a million-dollar lottery said, had she known the future, "I'd have torn up that ticket, or put it in someone else's name."

Christians can help slow the rising tide of gambling fever in all forms. And the first step is to educate law makers both by letter and by organizing committees. Thanks to an interdenominational church-led coalition in New Jersey a move to legalize casino gambling throughout the entire state was blocked several times by God's people.

Christians were again at the forefront of action recently in Indiana where an effort to legalize gambling was turned down in March 1985. The efforts of Indiana Citizens Against Legalized Gambling, a non-profit organization which attracted many Christians and the support of major denominations, gained the support of all four former living governors in opposing the legislation.

It was also the same citizens group that played a key role in the Indiana Supreme Court ruling that para-mutual betting is a form of an illegal lottery after the General Assembly had approved that type of gambling.

Christians can also meet with newspaper editors and write to newspapers to oppose attempts to bring gambling to their states. In Indiana, Russ Pulliam, a Christian and an editor for the *Indianapolis News*, wrote a number of effective editorials which helped shape public opinion in the state.

Anti-gambling forces should also continue to cite the track record of Atlantic City and how the influx of casinos has hurt the city and its people. This has already been done with success in defeating gambling referenda in Louisiana, West Virginia, Galveston, Texas and in Florida.

And it is always worthwhile to tell your elected officials that you don't want your cities destroyed by gambling. And be ready to cite facts, which are hard to ignore.

Former Colorado Gov. Richard Lamm opposed an attractive-sounding constitutional amendment to legalize casino gambling on a 4,300-acres site near Pueblo, Colo. on the basis that it would attract prostitution and crime.

In Arkansas, Gov. Bill Clinton opposed a proposal for casinos in Hot Springs, as did Hot Springs Mayor Jim Randall, who said the casinos would destroy a 20-year effort to make the spa a family-oriented attraction.

Christians should pray for God's leading in opportunities to oppose the further influx of gambling. We must ask ourselves some pointed questions. Is it biblical to rely on "luck" as a way out of poverty or to insure that you will never have to work again? It is right to profit from something at a great expense to others? Are we caring for our fellow human beings by encouraging them to gamble? An overview of scripture seems to indicate an emphatic no!

Discussion Questions

1. What, if anything, is wrong with wanting to get rich quick?

2. Do you feel Christians should be involved in raffles, sports pools, bingo for cash, etc. Why? Why not?

3. If gambling is addictive like drugs and alcohol, what can we as concerned individuals do to help people who struggle with this temptation?

4. Does your state have a lottery? What sort of people have you observed buying tickets?

5. How would you respond to the statement: "A person is responsible for his own choices. It's not my fault if he buys a lottery ticket when he can't afford it."

6. If you ever bought a $1 lottery ticket or put a quarter in a slot machine, how did you feel (a) if you won a few dollars, or (b) if you lost the money?

7. How would you respond to the statement, "The lottery is great for the state. It brings in a lot of money for education—and I don't have to pay as much in taxes"?

8. Do you believe that gambling—even in small, regulated doses—leads to more? Why? Why not?

CHAPTER 5

Consequences of the Sexual Revolution

A funny thing happened on the way to sexual utopia. We got burned. Clearly something has gone wrong with America's sexual revolution, so wrong that even the secular elite are grumbling about its broken promises.

A former advocate of the new morality, George Leonard, wrote "The End of Sex" for *Esquire* magazine in which he admitted, "the sexual revolution, in slaying some loathsome old dragons, has created some formidable new ones."

And therapist George Marin proclaimed in *Psychology Today*, "all of us must acknowledge, however reluctantly, that there was something to those 'reactionaries'...who argued that deliberate, broad changes in our systems of sexual remissions and taboos would let loose among us as many troubles as they solved."

R. Michael Sigler *is associate pastor of Gadsden Street United Methodist Church in Pensacola, Florida. He has an master's degree in communications from Wheaton College, Wheaton, Illinois.*

Most Christians in the 1960s and 1970s survived each new shock wave of the sexual revolution with mixed response. First came astonishment and, occasionally, outrage. Then came resignation: *Too bad, but the pendulum keeps swinging.*

It's hard to see history clearly when it's happening all around you. But things are different today. After 20 years of the new morality, its effects are beginning to sort themselves out. It is time to get an aerial view. Just where has this social experiment brought us, and where will we go from here?

Caught as we are in the post-revolutionary landscape of the 1980s, when out-of-wedlock sex has all the shock value of a late-night refrigerator raid, it is easy to forget just how far things have come, and how fast.

Some observers have noted signs of the emerging revolution as early as the 1920s, when the "flappers" created a stir with their short skirts and fast lifestyles. Sigmund Freud's influence also was being felt in the first half of this century. The belief was spreading that the true evil is sexual repression, not unrestrained expression. Sex was beginning to move outside the realm of the moral and religious and into the domain of science.

In the 1950s the Kinsey reports on sexual behavior in America created the impression that society's presumed adherence to traditional secular mores was a sham. Kinsey's studies portrayed an America in which three-quarters of the men and half of the women engaged in premarital sex. In Kinsey's America, half of the married men and one-fourth of the married women had extra-marital affairs.

Some critics today believe Kinsey drew from an unrepresentative sample so his reports exaggerated the level of moral looseness. Whether or not Kinsey's findings accurately reflected society as a whole, Americans got the message— "everybody *else* is doing it." Pre-marital and extra-marital sex lost some of its stigma.

Nevertheless, in spite of these sporadic blips on the morality monitor, traditional moral values held sway. Then came the 1960s.

It is not coincidental that the year which began the decade is when the birth-control pill became generally available. Penicillin and the pill disarmed advocates of traditional morality. No longer, it seemed, could the threat of venereal disease and unwanted pregnancy be held up as inducements to chastity.

It is difficult to fully appreciate the revolutionary nature of the new climate that moved in with the 1960s. The Kinsey studies had implied failure to live up to the generally accepted sexual ethic. But now *the ethic itself* was tossed to the winds. By the mid-to-late-1960s, society had lost any consensus regarding premarital sex, marital fidelity, obscenity and perversion.

The New Morality

Popular culture and its media touted the new sexual ethic from New York and L. A. to the Bible Belt. Sex before marriage was championed in pop music with songs like the Rolling Stones' "Let's Spend the Night Together," and on the screen with youth-targeted movies like "Love Story." The courts' inability to define obscenity invited a flood of sexually explicit films, books and magazines.

On June 29, 1970, 10,000 homosexuals gathered in New York City and marched down Sixth Avenue to Central Park, chanting: "Two, four, six, eight! Gay is just as good as straight!" and "Out of the closets! Into the streets!" The event marked the beginning of the gay rights movement in America.

And where was the Church during all this? The answer is that a significant part of the Church was racing to keep up with the revolution.

In 1965 a distinguished group of Protestant clergymen met at Harvard to ponder the new morality. They could agree on no definitive conclusions. But the general consensus seemed to favor some version of participant Joseph Fletcher's approach, known today as "situation ethics."

Fletcher argued that the Church should never absolutely condemn any sexual relationship. "The core proposition of the new morality," argued Fletcher, is that "there is only one thing which is always good regardless of circumstances, and that is neighborly concern, social responsibility, *agape*—which is a divine imperative." In this approach "one enters into every decision-making moment armed with all the wisdom of the culture, but prepared in one's freedom to suspend and violate any rule except that one must as responsibly as possible seek the good of one's neighbor."

In its coverage of the Harvard meeting, *Time* included the above quote followed by this editorial comment: "...quite a long thought for an 18-year-old during a passionate moment in the back seat of a car!"

From today's vantage point not only does situation ethics appear "quite a long thought" but an inadequate one as well. The same could be said about most of the sexual revolution's promises. Casting off outmoded restraints was supposed to set us free. Permissiveness would create a climate where the ugly, destructive side of sex—purged of false fear and guilt—would vanish. Instead this is what happened:

* Every year the average American teenager will log 2,500 hours of TV-viewing on the way to the 15,000 hours he'll see before high school graduation. He will watch an endless array of scenes depicting or suggesting sexual intercourse. And four out of five of these scenes will involve characters who are not married to each other.

* Between seventh and twelfth grades, this teenager will also listen to an estimated 10,500 hours of rock music—only 500 hours less than the total time he spends in 12 years of school. Along with some harmless tunes, he'll hear songs about topics such as incest and illicit sexual behavior.

* This high school student will attend sex education classes where he will learn the biological facts of sex and how to obtain and use contraceptives. He will not receive any advice on how to make moral decisions about sex.

Each year, in spite of the unprecedented emphasis on sex education, one out of every 10 teenage girls will get pregnant.

"Epidemic" is the word most frequently used to describe the situation. If present trends continue, researchers estimate that 40 percent of today's 14-year-old girls will be pregnant at least once before they reach age 20.

* Abortion has become one of the most common surgical procedures in America. Every year an estimated 1.6 million babies will be burned, chopped and suctioned from their mothers' wombs so that "love" can be "free."

* Many parents are afraid to leave their children with a sitter, in light of increasing reports of child abuse. "By even the most conservative estimates," says Christopher Dodd, chairman of the Senate Caucus On Children, "a child is sexually abused somewhere in this country *every two minutes.*"

* Americans will spend about eight billion dollars on pornographic products each year, and at least half of that money will go to organized crime. Among those who will help pay for this so-called victimless crime are the 300,000 children and young people used to pose for some 260 child-pornography, or "kiddie porn," magazines. Among the magazines' readers will be members of the Rene Guyon Society, which seeks the legalization of sex between adults and children, and NAMBLA—the North American Man-Boy Love Association.

* 1.5 million American women are raped each year. The rape rate in the United States has increased by more than 700 percent since 1933.

* A well-organized and politically powerful homosexual movement will continue its efforts to gain unconditional acceptance of the homosexual lifestyle. Meanwhile, the number of AIDS cases continues to increase at an alarming rate. So far, there is no cure for this inevitably fatal disease.

* Among heterosexuals, the sexually promiscuous may be a bit more selective in their choice of partners. A new epidemic of sexually transmitted diseases (STDs) with names such as herpes and chlamydia hit this country in the 1970s and continues to date.

Medical experts estimate that 27,000 new cases of STDs occur daily, and that if present trends continue, 25 percent of all

Americans between age 15 and 55 will be infected. Many of the 25 known diseases, including genital herpes, are incurable. Not only do they last for a lifetime, but they can be passed on to children during birth.

Psychological Costs of the New Morality

Add to this legacy a host of less visible but equally devastating results—including the *psychological* and *relational* bills that are coming due.

Dr. David Seamands, a former local church pastor whose ministry in emotional healing is reaching a wide audience through books such as his best-selling *Healing for Damaged Emotions*, counsels many people affected by today's sexually permissive climate. He tells of a young woman who came to him for marriage counseling. In one session, he asked her how many different men she had slept with before her present marriage. "She was hard pressed to come up with a number," Seamands recalls, "but finally she said the number of sexual partners must have been around 60 to 80.

"I will always remember her next statement: 'You know, Doc, I've given away so many pieces of myself. I feel like I have nothing more to give, nothing left to give my husband.'"

The cost of America's sexual revolution, then, must be counted not only in terms of disease epidemics and runaway teen-pregnancy rates. Couples and families pay too, as they're ripped apart by infidelity, divorce and serial remarriage.

That is where we have come. The bigger issue now is what it all means, and where we go from here.

Lurking behind all the talk about broken promises and post-revolutionary fallout is a basic but heavily loaded question: *Is this the judgment of God?*

The question kept coming up in the popular media—especially in regard to the AIDS epidemic—long before the Church ever said much about it. Time and again as pundit or power broker aired his views on the matter, somewhere out of the subliminal mists arose a comment like this: "Of course *some* people will see this as divine judgment or a vindication of the Judeo-Christian ethic." Unstated conclusion: "How dare they!"

How dare they indeed. Humanistic philosophy and technological know-how had started this revolution, and they would take care of its problems. God and religion, keep quiet!

Eventually, Church leaders did begin to speak. A bishop in New York announced categorically, "AIDS is not God's judgment." The idea of God punishing "so-called sins," said the bishop, comes from "primitive, barbaric passages of the Old Testament." A TV evangelist jumped in to argue to the contrary.

Most people have preferred just to dismiss the question. But it deserves an answer. For in the long run, our approach to the current sexual crisis may come down to this:

If we live in a morally neutral universe, pills and penicillin should decide the matter. Our present difficulties may mean we need better sex education and some new wonder drugs, but not a different sexual ethic.

If, however, as Christianity teaches, we live in a world with morality written into the nature of things, then this crisis is the inevitable consequence of siding against a moral universe. As Methodist missionary and evangelist E. Stanley Jones said, "You are free to choose, but you are not free to choose the results or consequences of your choices....You do not break these laws written into the nature of things; you break yourselves on them."

We recoil from the idea of judgment because we dislike the idea of a tyrannical God hurling lightning bolts, or AIDS viruses, at us when we step out of line. But we have no trouble accepting the fact that our automobiles will self-destruct if we drive them without oil. Likewise, as C. S. Lewis reminds us, "Moral rules are directions for running the human machine. Every moral rule is there to prevent a breakdown, or a strain, or a friction, in the running of that machine."

A government agency interviewed 50 homosexual AIDS patients. It found that the median number of sexual partners over a lifetime was 1,150. There are consequences to such a lifestyle.

Jesus, we should remember, had as much to say about judgment as He did about love. He knew the offer of grace had no meaning apart from the understanding that all people are moving toward judgment—perhaps during this life, but assuredly in the one to come. Grace is God's antidote to judgment—and judgment in this life may be God's tender mercies in disguise.

Reconsidering the New Morality

The implications lead to some potentially *good* news in all this: *Might not our society, after two decades of wandering in this sexual wilderness, be ready to reconsider the new morality?*

The ugly fruits of America's sexual revolution—AIDS, child abuse, and the like—may be putting the brakes on our headlong skid into moral nihilism. And another less dramatic but perhaps more significant force is at work in the kind of disillusionment and reevaluation expressed by Marin:

"The sexual freedom established during the past couple of decades," says Marin, "has not been accompanied by the increase in happiness that many people assumed would follow from a freeing of sexual mores.... We have been liberated from the taboos of the past only to find ourselves imprisoned in a 'freedom' that brings us no closer to our real nature or needs."

While the inadequacies of the new morality are becoming increasingly clear, a growing body of evidence is giving support to the Christian sexual ethic. Several years ago *Redbook* magazine questioned 100,000 American women about their sex lives. It was the most extensive survey of female sexuality since Kinsey's studies. The most astonishing finding was the discovery of a direct link between sexual satisfaction and religious commitment. The survey showed that no matter what the age, education or income of respondents, women who described themselves as "strongly religious" were far more likely to describe their sex lives as highly satisfying than were their non-religious counterparts.

Notes Dr. Seamands, "The notion that Christians are repressed and Victorian is a myth. The fact is that a Christian marriage provides the security that couples need for maximum sexual freedom and enjoyment."

Recent studies are disproving the myth that living together before the wedding improves marriage. The new evidence suggests that precisely the opposite is true, and exposes yet another broken promise of the sexual revolution.

We are living in a day when the consequences of the last two decades are becoming increasingly apparent. What will be the result?

One would like to predict society's full-scale retreat from sexual permissiveness, but the new morality is for now well-entrenched. As the negative consequences amass, its advocates may reject some of the extremes of the sexual revolution. But supporters are unlikely to walk away from its basic propositions, whose roots grow deep in the philosophical soil of moral relativism.

Nevertheless, we seem to have entered a critical phase in America's sex saga, a time when minds may be more open to Christian ethical alternatives.

How, then, should we respond to these times?

1. *Strengthen our own foundations.* The distressing fact about the Church's response to the sexual revolution is this: we too often have sold our sexual birthright for a mess of secular pottage. A study done by the American Lutheran Church, for example, showed that an average of 40 percent of that church's couples live together before marriage. Other denominations may not be far behind.

It's time the Church quit following society and start leading it. If ever we needed experiential evidence to confirm the sexual ethic presented in scripture, we are getting it now! It's time the Church repent of its capitulation to what has been rightly called, not the new morality, but "the old immorality."

Christians in the wake of society's sexual revolution must reclaim God's good gift of sexuality. The Church must do more to strengthen marriages and affirm the goodness of human sexuality as expressed within God-given boundaries. The Marriage Enrichment and Engaged Discovery movements are encouraging examples of what can be done.

The walking wounded of the revolution, both within and without of the Church fold, must be loved and ministered to. But the call to repentance must not be ignored. Jesus was a friend to prostitutes and thieves. The early church offered fornicators, adulterers and homosexuals the right hand of fellowship, *as* they turned from those lifestyles— "such *were* some of you" (1 Corinthians 6:11).

As for our own day, Francis Schaeffer was correct when he said we are living in a post-Christian era. The Church may have to live a long time yet in a society committed to moral relativism and sexual permissiveness. We need to strengthen our own foundations in order to stand against the shifting winds of culture.

At the same time, there is a growing awareness out there that the new morality is not all it promised to be. In this period of transition and reevaluation, Christian people should discern the times and seize the initiative.

2. *Speak up and reach out.* "Making an open stand against all the ungodliness and unrighteousness which overspread our land as a flood is one of the noblest ways of confessing Christ in the face of His enemies." John Wesley, the founder of Methodism, spoke these words during a time in England when that nation's moral decline rivaled America's today. Historian Harold Nicholson described the beginning of John Wesley's era as "a period of moral disorder."

How did Wesley respond? He "did not waste his time deploring the evils of his day," notes Richard Pyke, "he attacked them; and he attacked them by preaching repentance and conversion. He knew that *the only hope of the corrupt heart is a new birth."*

As the sexual revolution's disastrous effects hit home, reform initiatives are arising on several fronts. The right-to-life movement and a growing opposition to sexploitation in the media are two examples. Christians should be on the front lines of such efforts. But we must also remember that activism alone is never adequate. As we speak up, we must also reach out—in word and deed—with the love of Jesus Christ.

Outreach and the New Morality

Evangelism research shows that individuals respond to the Gospel most readily during times of crisis or transition. Today's Church has the opportunity to offer a generation weary of wandering in a sexual wasteland not only a better way of life but also the One who *is* the way and the life.

Chuck Colson told about a young woman on his staff named Christy who, along with members of her prayer group, began to visit terminally-ill AIDS patients. Most of the patients received few visits, even from family. Christy's group spent evenings and weekends with the patients, taking stationery, postage stamps, books, tapes, cookies.

In a prayer memo, Christy explained why. "They are scared. They are dying. They are unsaved....We have been able to pray with eight of the patients," she added. "Two men who died in the last ten days received Christ. We've had in-depth conversations with one man about Jesus, the Good News, sin, justification, and repentance."

Someone asked Christy if she was afraid. "No," she replied, "we believe we are doing the will of God" (*Who Speaks for God?* p. 22).

There are encouraging signs that many other Christians are catching such a vision. I've seen them in my own community.

A fellow employee and his wife became foster parents of a 14-year-old victim of child abuse.

My brother spent a Saturday walking a picket line in front of a store that sells pornography.

Another friend is an outspoken advocate of the right-to-life cause. She and her husband welcomed a teenaged girl into their home, and she was pregnant and unmarried. They helped her through the child's birth and prearranged adoption by a childless Christian couple.

These are not characters in an inspirational novel. They are ordinary Christians. And their numbers are growing—ordinary Christians who've decided to do something about America's moral landslide and its destructive fallout.

They are speaking out, taking a stand. They are also channeling their indignation into sacrificial service for Jesus Christ by helping hurting people. Like Christy, they believe this to be the will of God. And they see that *now* is the time to do it.

Discussion Questions

1. How would you define the sexual revolution?

2. What are the physical consequences of the sexual revolution? The emotional consequences? The spiritual consequences?

3. Do you agree with the C.S. Lewis quote: "Moral rules are directions for running the human machine. Every moral rule is there to prevent a breakdown, or a strain, or a friction, in the running of that machine"? Why? Why not?

4. How would you respond to a person who asks, "Why is it so important that people limit sexual activity to marriage if they love each other and take steps to prevent pregnancy and disease?"

5. How would you answer a person who asks, "Why doesn't God want me to enjoy life?"

6. What would you say to a person who feels guilt over sexual misconduct?

7. Think back over the past 10 years. How has your perspective on sexual values changed?

8. What can you do to prevent being conformed to the world's sexual values? How can you help your children or grandchildren who feel pressured to adopt society's standards?

CHAPTER 6

Obedience in the "Little Things"

I admit to some recent reactions of which I am not proud.

A. I was in a hurry and not at all happy when a car pulled out in front of me while I was driving home. I laid on the horn to show my displeasure, and when I had a chance passed the car with a roar, glared at the driver and spoke a few choice words, making sure the driver saw my lips moving. Only then did I realize the driver of the other car was a parishioner, a dear saint (whether she could drive or not), with whom I had had prayer on a number of occasions. I experienced what might best be described as instant conviction and sensed that my sanctification was not nearly as complete as it might be. But why—I think now upon reflection—did it matter whether the person was somebody I knew or did not know?

Riley B. Case *is a United Methodist Minister and a district superintendent for the Marion Indiana Conference. He received an honorary doctorate from Taylor University, Marion, Indiana.*

B. I had a note to call a person but didn't get around to making the call for a number of days. I had tried at least once, or at least thought I had. At any rate, when I finally made the call I found myself saying "I have been trying to return your call but have not gotten through to you." Once again, a quick rush of conviction. I had lied, or at least had shaded the truth greatly, to make myself look not so irresponsible.

C. The restaurant was understaffed, so the waitress was overworked and harried. When she finally came to take my order I said (unkindly and without thinking), "You folks around here evidently don't believe in service." I spent the rest of the meal hoping she wouldn't find out I claimed to be a Christian.

In none of these instances was I guilty of what might be called a major moral lapse, but these *were* moral lapses all the same. And they serve as reminders to me that it is usually not in the "big" issues that I am often insensitive and need help, but in the "little things," everyday relationships, attitudes and habits.

It is to the everyday "little things" that the Bible directs a great deal of attention. The book of Proverbs, for example, is full of advice on how God wants everyday life to be ordered: "A gentle answer turns away wrath" (15:1); "Honor the Lord from your wealth" (3:9); "Do not contend with a man without cause, if he has done you no harm" (3:30); "Put away from you a deceitful mouth" (4:24); "A slothful man does not roast his prey" (12:27).

Much of the New Testament teaching continues this same kind of practical advice. "Do not speak against one another" (James 4:11); "Do not be haughty in mind, but associate with the lowly" (Romans 12:16); "Be anxious for nothing" (Phil. 4:6); "Have this attitude in yourselves, which was also in Christ Jesus" (Phil. 2:5).

Morality, Culture and "Little Things"

With the biblical emphasis before us, and keeping in mind some of the challenges of our present culture and the age in which we live, let us consider several principles in the discussion of a "Morality of Little Things."

1. At the very minimum a Christian morality of little things means good manners and basic integrity. There are certain values that we urge upon all people, whether they are Christian or not. These include such things as respect for others, truthfulness, kindness, fair play, and the honoring of commitments.

This seems so elementary, yet I can think of many instances where a Christian testimony has been undermined by a lapse in basic manners:

a. A factory worker who reads his Bible during break time but is not friendly enough even to greet his fellow workers with a pleasant "good morning."

b. A man who talks too much.

c. A woman who lets her dog run loose in the neighborhood even though this is highly offensive to the neighbors.

Some of us were reared in homes where basic manners and respect were taught. But some of us were not, and we need to learn it as adults. This means we start with learning the words "please" and "thank you." This means we learn how to express gratitude, how to be pleasant on the phone, how to be gracious in conversation. This means we answer when spoken to, do not habitually show up late for meetings, dress appropriately and do not crowd in front of others at the check-out lane in the supermarket.

2. But having said this, a Christian morality of little things must go beyond manners and even the best of the values of the world around us. This is the whole point of the Sermon on the Mount (Matthew 5-7). The Sermon on the Mount might be called a modern manual on ethics for believers. We might also call it "second-mile" morality. "If any one forces you to go one mile, go with him two miles" (Mt. 5:41). Good manners ask that we treat people with respect and give honor to whom honor is due. Second-mile morality asks that we go beyond respect with love and forgiveness. If we are cursed, we bless in return. If we are criticized and misunderstood, we do not seek to defend ourselves. If we are wronged, we do not return vengeance but forgiveness.

We might also call this "Good Samaritan" morality. The Good Samaritan did not have to help the man beaten and left for dead, but he did. So are we to do in second-mile morality.

I do not think I ever doubted Christianity because of the argument of atheists, but I did have some doubts as a little boy when a "Christian" neighbor gave me a good swift kick (literally) when I ran across his newly-seeded lawn to retrieve a baseball. He pointed out in his angry lecture that he had warned us not to walk on the grass, and that I was a nuisance to the neighborhood. That might well have been true, but I remember in my little-boy logic, thinking, *but he's a Christian and he shouldn't do that.* That logic is not to be faulted. God expects more of His children than of the world around us.

3. We do not naturally and normally live out second-mile morality. It grows out of a Spirit-filled walk with Christ, with an effort to be faithful to the New Testament regardless of how others act or believe.

It is quite possible that God would lead some of us to take moral stands that are not only unusual because of the world around us but are controversial even in the Christian community. In the home in which I grew up guns were not allowed. This was because guns suggested war and killing and violence, and that seemed inconsistent with peacemaking and the Sermon on the Mount. It did not matter that guns were found in other church-going homes. Our home was to be different. When I was old enough to go to movies I was allowed only to go to "good" movies, which meant movies that did not show people drinking alcoholic beverages or fighting or shooting each other (which eliminated most of the movies). However much I complained at the time, I am thankful for that emphasis today.

The point is that those moral decisions went against the grain, not only of the society around us but also of other church families. That did not mean that we were "Christian" and they were not, or that we were right and they were wrong. But it did mean that we (or at least my parents) took seriously a Christian morality that went further than what was common in the culture around us.

I know of families who choose not to have a TV set or who limit the amount of time spent watching TV. I know of other persons who have quit jobs out of sympathy for a co-worker who was mistreated, or who were fired because they would not cover-up for a boss who was dishonest in business. I know of persons who out of commitment to Christ have pledged with themselves never to speak ill of another person, and others who have pledged themselves to triple-tithe their income to the Lord's work out of obedience to Christ.

This morality is not a matter of following the course of least resistance, but it represents a deliberate and intentional decision to go the second mile in a morality of little things.

Grace and Humor

4. We always live by grace. We should add that we must also live by good humor. Unfortunately, serving Christ in the little things, what we have called second-mile morality, easily falls into phariseeism and perfectionism. The sin of the Pharisees was not too many rules but their rigidity in putting rules before people. To put it another way, they were mean-spirited and betrayed the very law they sought to uphold. Christians ought to be fun to be with. If we are seen as negative and judgmental we have missed the purpose of serving Christ.

It takes a great deal of grace to stand against alcohol and yet love the alcoholic, or to speak against the practice of homosexuality as a legitimate lifestyle and still love the homosexual, or to associate with obnoxious people without showing disgust. But that's what Christ asks us to do.

And yet this is not what saves us. That point must be made over and over. Our second-mile morality is not what makes us rightly related to God—that comes only through the merits of Jesus Christ. Our morality is the working-out of our salvation. And because our standards are so high we are continually susceptible to a sense of failure, which in turn leads to low self-esteem. As many wise Christian counselors will testify, the most common emotional problem among evangelical Christians is low self-esteem, coming often from perfectionism.

In response we must hold always to the truth: we are accepted by God only through the shed blood of Jesus Christ by faith, not by works. We are loved not because of what we do and what we attain but because of who Christ is. However, because we are loved we want to please the One who loves us. Our love works itself out even in the most difficult areas of life, in the little things.

Discussion Questions

What would you do in these situations?

1. I am secretary of my club and enjoy my job very much. Part of my responsibility is to send notices of the meetings to all the members. On one occasion I prepared the notices and gave them to the president because she said she would mail them, but she forgot. On another occasion she did not tell me when there was a special meeting, so no one received notices. I hear now that the club may elect a new secretary because I have not been doing my job. Should I put the blame where it really belongs? (Matthew 5:38-42).

2. I am starting a new business. For the past two years I have worked 65-70 hours a week. The business has been successful but my wife complains that I am never at home. There is a good chance that I could become very successful so that not only would I have more money to help others but influence in the community would be great. Should I continue as I have or cut back my hours? (Matthew 6:19-21).

3. The teacher in my daughter's Sunday school class taught a lesson on sharing with the poor and suggested that most people spend money selfishly, like for shoes they don't really need. The next day when I said I was interested in the shoe sale at the department store at the mall, my daughter told me she had counted 20 pairs of shoes in my closet, and did I really need more shoes. We already tithe our income. What shall I say to my daughter? (Matthew 6:25-33).

4. While our family was out for a walk one Sunday afternoon we passed the neighbor's orchard and I picked up some apples from the ground to eat. That night when I was putting my son to bed he said "Daddy we stole some apples from Mr. Brown today, didn't we?" What shall I say to my son? (Matthew 5:14-16, 37).

CHAPTER 7

You *Can* Do Something About Pornography!

The release of Attorney General Ed Meese's pornography commission report in 1986 brought pornography to the attention of thousands of Christians who hadn't given the subject much thought or taken it seriously.

Up until three years before the controversial report, I had never heard an explicit discussion on pornography and my responsibility to do something about it.

In 1983 I attended the first National Consultation on Pornography and Obscenity held in Cincinnati, Ohio. Since that

---

Paul A. Tanner *is Executive Secretary of the Executive Council for the Church of God (Anderson, Indiana). He is a cabinet member of the National Coalition Against Pornography and a member of the Advisory Board of the National Federation for Decency.*

time I have seen too much, I have read too much, and now I know too much. I can no longer sit idly by and watch an 8-billion-dollar smut industry devour our children, demean our women and destroy our family values.

Since that meeting I have mobilized 2,300 congregations in my denomination, the Church of God (Anderson, Indiana). I have led the formation of a highly effective anti-pornography organization in the city where I live. I have worked on the pornography issue in dozens of community structures, denominational bodies, service clubs and inter-church organizations.

Obviously I feel that the role of the Church is to influence our society. Jesus used the words "salt," "light" and "leaven" to describe the effect His people are to have on the world.

What has happened to America's social structures since the advent of the *Playboy* philosophy in 1955? In my lifetime we have gone from silent movies downtown to hard-core downstairs. We're not talking about a few pictures of semi-nude women.

We're talking about an 8-billion-dollar-a-year industry. This country has 15,000 "adult" bookstores containing more than 200,000 private viewing booths that charge 25 cents per minute. The industry has moved far beyond nudity to simulated sex, oral sex, homosexuality, bestiality, group orgies and now kiddie porn, featuring children 6 and 7 years of age.

We're talking about 20 million magazines a month. *Penthouse* alone produces 4,000 per hour. There are more than 450 different pornographic periodicals, enough every year to pave a two-lane highway, with covers alone, from Washington, D.C. to San Francisco.

We're talking about books with such titles as *Anal Games With My Sister, I Took My Bra Off For Daddy, A Manual For Rape* and *Lust For Fun.*

We're talking about hard-rock music performed by musicians who wear belts, chains, leather whips and other sadomasochistic imagery while singing filthy lyrics about pain, bondage, violence and sexual abuse.

You Can Do Something About Pornography! 73

We're talking about organizations whose sole purpose is the use and abuse of children: Rene Guyon Society. NAMBLA (North American Man-Boy Love Association). These are pedophile organizations that advocate a repeal of the "age of consent" law. Ken Wooden of ABC's "20/20" reports that the average child molester will abuse 366 children in his or her lifetime.

It's not just the 250 "kiddie porn" publications that hurt children. The supposedly "soft-core" magazines now glorify child sexual abuse. Every month, *Hustler* magazine features a full-page cartoon, "Chester the Molester." *Hustler* advertises vinyl-rubber, child-size boy and girl dolls with sexual parts for use in mechanical copulation. Pictures of women in bondage and torture, in every form of subordination, degradation and sadomasochism are now common in the supposedly harmless "soft-core" magazines.

A million children run away every year and more than 30 percent of them become child prostitutes. Children are bought and sold like so much merchandise. But how do eight-month-old babies, gagging with gonorrhea of the throat, escape from parents who force them into bizarre sex acts—with each other, with adults and with animals—in front of a camera, and then sell the pictures to the smut peddler?

America is experiencing a sexual holocaust. Pornographers don't know when to stop and they won't until they are confronted by people who care enough to stand up and say, "Enough is enough." We must remove this malignancy from the life of American society.

A society cannot promote a morality on the level of stray dogs—sex anywhere, anytime, with anyone—and not reap the consequences. Sodom and Gomorrah did not escape. Neither did Rome. And neither will America.

One out of every 10 teenage girls in America is pregnant. That's two to seven times higher than in any other developed country. As many as 600,000 babies are born to unwed teenagers every year.

In a study of 940 adult women, 48 percent—nearly one half—reported at least one unwanted sexual experience with a relative, involving physical contact, before the age of 14.

According to an NBC television film, child sexual abuse in America has tripled in the last generation. Genital herpes has increased from 500,000, 20 years ago, to 20 million, and another 500,000 cases are added every year.

Each year more babies will be affected by sexually-transmitted diseases than contracted polio during the entire epidemic of the 1950s.

In 1979 there were only nine known cases of AIDS. By the mid 80s, 15,000 had died of the dread disease.

What Should the Church Do?

What appropriate social action should the Church be taking to safeguard the physical, moral and spiritual well-being of our women and children?

1. *Establish parameters and sharpen the focus.* If we are to change the face of America, the goal must be so stated as to receive broad consensus from all church denominations. Our objective must not be exclusively moralistic. We must avoid either being, or being perceived as, religious or political extremists. Specifically our goal should be to: *remove all pornography which involves or affects children, and depicts the graphic, sexually-explicit subordination and degradation of women.*

Such a goal would get broad consensus from virtually every segment of our population, including the media. Tens of thousands of Americans would readily support this focus. As a byproduct, they would begin to view all pornography through different eyes.

For many decency advocates this goal does not go far enough. I know, because I am one of them. Their agendas call for specific action on homosexuality, extramarital activity, abortion and other related issues. But I can lay aside my personal agenda for the time being in order to cooperate with the whole Body of Christ in achieving *this* goal. If we unite, this is a battle that can be won!

You Can Do Something About Pornography! 75

2. *We must get the message to the mainline denominations.* Since the first National Consultation many smaller denominational groups have launched church-wide efforts. But the numbers are not sufficient to effectively make an impact on the pornography plague in America. It's not enough that 8,000 stores have removed pornographic magazines or that *Playboy's* circulation has dropped from seven million to four million since 1972.

The National Coalition Against Pornography (N-CAP) has already endorsed this focus. The organization has engaged a national advertising and marketing firm to give widespread publicity and media coverage to this concern.

N-CAP is eager to work with every denomination that will join them in their specific goal to "remove all pornography which involves or affects children and pornography which depicts the graphic, sexually-explicit subordination and degradation of women."

We will use every platform available to get this message to the hierarchy of every denomination in America. Denominational leaders must come to know the impact of pornography on our children, our wives and our mothers. The word must pass down through the denominational system to every pulpit and eventually to every person in the pew.

3. *We need to mobilize every community.* Our organizational efforts should be citizen-based rather than church-based. If every congregation will raise its voice in united concern, there will be enough sensitivity that we can unite and make progress at the local level. The Church has the largest task force potential in America. We can do anything that needs doing, that we really want done—if we are informed, if we care and if we are not afraid.

Our thrust will be so pervasive that we will get media attention and our focus so reasonable that we will get media support. The Church, however, must seize the initiative if it is to become an agent of change for America.

The need for *community* organization is because the Supreme Court has declared that "Obscenity shall be determined by community standards." Every community has a constitutional right to promote and maintain its own standard of decency. For example, if Los Angeles or Houston were to choose to have X-rated movies, adult book stores or nude beaches, that does not have to be the standard for the city where you live.

Cincinnati has determined that adult book stores and X-rated movies are not consistent with the community's values. The courts have supported this position and Cincinnati doesn't have a single X-rated movie theater or adult book store. Neither does Atlanta. And you don't have to have them where you live, unless you want them.

4. *We must demand the stern enforcement of laws prohibiting the sexual exploitation of women and children.* The advocates of decency are often charged with taking away liberty and freedom of speech. We are accused of censorship and undermining the Bill of Rights and the American way of life. *Penthouse* has carried full-page ads in newspapers and on it's own pages asking readers to stand up and speak out against decency advocates before it is too late.

Pro-pornography Arguments

The four most common counter-attacks by pornographers are as follows:

1. "Selling pornography is a First Amendment right." Quite the contrary. Throughout our history there have been laws regulating obscenity. People have never had the right to publicly distribute such material.

The idea that our forefathers intended to defend traffic in obscene material when they chose to protect freedom of speech is patent nonsense. Freedom of speech secures the right of dissent, civil discourse and intellectual communication. Speech is cognitive. Obscenity has no cognitive content. The Supreme Court has held that obscenity, the depiction of sex acts, is not speech and therefore has no part of civil or intellectual discourse.

Those who claim First Amendment immunity for their degenerate wares are attempting to confuse the public.

Pornography is not a First Amendment *right,* it is a civil *wrong.* It is outside the protection of the First Amendment just as libel, slander and perjury are outside its protection.

2. Pornographers tell us that "you can't legislate morality." Let's think that one through. Is not our whole judicial system based on the Ten Commandments? Almost every law legislates morality in some manner. Every law sets forth some standard for its citizens.

It is true, we cannot legislate *spirituality.* We cannot make people love what is right. But we certainly can make them obey what is right.

Some whites hate blacks. No law can make people love each other. But can blacks expect legal protection from bigoted whites? They can and have. Women, likewise, should expect the protection of the law from abusive men. We must see that such laws are enforced.

Private morals are private; public morals are public and are the business of community.

3. Advocates of decency are charged with "censorship." Censorship is "prior restraint" and the control of visual and literary material by an autocracy (one) or oligarchy (few). Since Gallup polls say that 80 percent of Americans oppose pornography, strong obscenity laws are inevitable.

Obscenity laws do not prohibit the printing of materials. But there are laws (postal, customs and transportation) which prohibit the circulation of obscene material. These laws represent the will of the people. The electorate has the right to establish its own standards. This is not censorship.

4. Another common response to decency advocates is, "Nobody has ever clearly defined pornography. We don't know what it is." Such arguments reflect an ignorance of current law. In 1973 the Supreme Court redefined "obscene" in the "Miller vs. California" case. Obscenity, ruled the court, is material meeting any of the following three criteria:

a. "Whether the average person, applying contemporary

community standards would find that the work, taken as a whole, appeals to the prurient interest;

b. whether the work depicts or describes, in a patently offensive way, sexual conduct specifically defined by the applicable state law; and

c. whether the work, taken as a whole, lacks serious literary, artistic, political or scientific value."

To leave no doubt as to what it had in mind, the court gave two examples of what guideline "b" means: "patently offensive representations or descriptions of ultimate sexual acts, normal or perverted, actual or simulated; and...of masturbation, excretory functions and lewd exhibition of the genitals."

The Church has a vital role to play in society with reference to pornography and violence, and I pray to God that we fill that role before it is too late.

Discussion Questions

1. What is a good working definition of pornography?

2. What do you understand to be some of the consequences to individuals and to society of widespread distribution of pornographic materials?

3. If someone were to honestly ask you, "What's all the fuss about? Why should I get upset about pornography?", what reasonable and intelligent answer would you give them?

4. How would you respond to someone who says, "You can't deny people the right to publish and read what they want"?

5. Do your local grocery or convenience stores carry "adult" magazines and videos that are readily available to minors? What could you do to express your displeasure?

6. An adult bookstore or X-rated theater opens in your neighborhood. Who would you call to protest? What other action could you take?

7. You find a pornographic magazine stuffed under your son's mattress. What would you say to him?

8. If someone were to say to you, "Fighting pornography is a dirty business. Christians should stay out of it," what would you say?

9. What could you do to encourage concerned church members to protest the spread of pornography in your community?

CHAPTER 8

Dismissing Racial Misconceptions

When most people think of racism, they associate it with cross burnings or rock throwing. Such incidents generate publicity, but most prejudice shows up in much more subtle and "civilized" ways. As a black person, I have experienced at least two significant incidents of racial prejudice that will be forever etched in my memory.

The first occurred while I was a high school senior. I had worked as hard as possible during high school, graduating with a B-plus average. Yet my white high school counselor advised me to enroll in a junior college. He said he didn't think I could succeed in a four-year institution without a junior college background.

Joseph Harris *is pastor of Quayle United Methodist Church in Oklahoma City, Oklahoma. He served as chairman of the Tulsa Human Rights Commission and as a member of the Urban League Housing Counseling Board. He earned his D.Min. from Oral Roberts University.*

Some years later I found he had recommended to every black student in my program that they attend a junior college or not attend college at all! I have since graduated from a four-year state university, seminary and doctoral programs.

The second incident was not so obvious. My family and I were members of a predominantly black church within a conservative, evangelical, predominantly white, Pentecostal denomination. But one thing about the church always bothered me—the policy which kept ethnic churches separate from white churches in most denominational events except a once-a-year camp meeting.

I asked my pastor and members of the white churches why this was so. My pastor, who was black, responded that the denomination did not have a policy against integrated churches but historical practices kept the races apart. When I asked members of the white churches about this, one said he felt that "you people" would be more comfortable worshiping in "your own" environment.

A pastor of one of the white churches said he felt integration would hinder church growth, adding that research indicated that people were more comfortable worshiping in homogeneous groupings.

After some time of prayer and consideration, my family left this denomination because of what we perceived to be an unintentional reinforcement of institutional racism and prejudice.

Both forms of prejudice I experienced were based upon race and presumptions about race. The actions which followed those presuppositions could have been damaging to me, my fellow high school students and members of our denomination. My strong family background, a good support system and a relationship with Christ prevented me from becoming injured emotionally. However, history is full of victims who were less fortunate, who took the wrong advice or who neglected to ask the right questions. As a result, they bear emotional scars, and many live unfulfilled lives.

Racism in all forms, inside and outside the church, poses one of the great moral dilemmas of our time. Although we think we can spot a prejudiced person, we often fail to recognize when *we* might be that person. Perhaps we do not feel racist compared to the klansmen. We are not as obvious about our prejudices as they are. Certainly we don't hate as they do. After all, our children go to school with blacks, we may work beside an ethnic minority person, and we may even live in the same neighborhood with minority families. Thus we determine we are not prejudiced because we are not "against" anybody.

Part of the reason we don't see our prejudicial attitudes could be that we lack an adequate definition of racism. We often fail to ask ourselves, "How am I prejudiced?" Webster defines racism as a belief that race is the primary determinant of human traits and capacities and that racial differences produce an inherent superiority of a particular race. Some black leaders have defined racism as the ability to exercise or yield power over an individual based on racial characteristics and stereotyping. They say because blacks are basically powerless, they cannot participate in racism.

The first definition is very sterile. The second may present an historically and sociologically accurate account of racial practices —it is certainly true that the unjust use of power based on racial criteria has been a characteristic of racism throughout history. Yet both definitions only describe symptoms of a deeper problem. For an accurate definition of racism we must turn to scripture.

An Accurate Definition

Scripture is clear that the root cause of all "ism's" lies in the sin of humanity. Classism, sexism and racism are a result of sin. Because of humanity's alienation from God, men and women became separated from their Creator and consequently from other human beings (Gen. 3:22-23). You could say that the remainder of the biblical witness is mankind's attempt to deal with sin and reconcile itself to God and to others (2 Cor. 5:18-20).

Assuming that this is correct, biblical history can be seen as humanity's successes and failures in the area of overcoming sin as individuals and as societies. We can look at our own success and failure in overcoming sin and readily see that conquering sin can be a process of winning and losing until victory is finally achieved.

Therefore when we describe the "ism's" in which people individually and corporately participate, we must see them as symptomatic of unrepented sin. That puts racism in the category of sin. Viewing racism as sin makes the Webster definition more dynamic and limits the definition used by some black leaders. For if racism is, as is all sin, no respecter of persons, then all human beings may be susceptible to committing the sin of racism. Blacks, Hispanics, Asians and others can be prejudiced against people of different races. The crucial factor here is that we define prejudice and racism as sins needing repentance as individuals, as a Church and as a society.

Peter's means of dealing with the problem remains the classic biblical example for us all. He emerged after Pentecost (Acts 2) as one of the prominent leaders of the new Christian community. Filled with the Holy Spirit and God's love through Christ, Peter zealously went out to build Christ's Church. In his zealousness, however, he became convinced that this meant building Christ's Church among the circumcised Jewish Christians.

Remaining loyal to the Jewish culture where he perceived it did not contradict his Christian beliefs, Peter had convinced himself culturally and prejudicially that the Church of Jesus Christ did not include Gentiles who would not submit to the Hebrew tradition of circumcision. After all, circumcision was a sign of faith in God expressed by Abraham and a symbolic agreement to adhere to cultural and ceremonial laws. Peter felt religiously justified in excluding Gentiles who confessed belief in Christ but were unwilling to submit to cultural and ceremonial requirements.

But God confronted Peter (Acts 10) in a vision about who and what he might or might not exclude because of man-made, cultural distinctions, and then He sent him to the home of a person Peter would have previously excluded from the Church (Acts

Dismissing Racial Misconceptions

10:19-20). Peter realized that he had been working from old prejudicial conceptions, culturally and religiously baptized, but nevertheless wrong. He concluded from this experience that God is no respecter of persons (v. 34).

Peter was Spirit-filled, respectable and probably felt he would never knowingly participate in a prejudicial act against anyone. But the subtle nature of the sin of prejudice can become so entrenched in an individual, group, culture or society that unless one is constantly sensitive to the warning signs of unconscious participation, one can easily be like Peter.

Learning from Peter and within the definition of racism as sin, there are several ways we can find victory in this area of our lives.

1. We can each do a self-inventory about our own racial attitudes. Ask yourself if you accept racial or ethnic stereotyping. Think about how would you feel if a member of a different racial or ethnic group:

moved next door,
worked alongside you,
went to school with your children,
was a member of your church,
dated your children,
married one of them.

2. Think about your willingness to be an advocate for the victims of racism as one might be an advocate for the victims of other sin-related issues. When evangelicals and others stand up for the victims of abortion, pornography or drug abuse, they are standing up for the victims of sin-related activities. The same fervor must accompany reaction against racism.

3. You can also look honestly at yourself and your family history to know if you need to repent and from what you need to repent. Were you reared in a family where racial characteristics were emphasized? As a child, did your role models reflect superior-inferior attitudes toward the races? Has your model of humanity subtly been determined by television, movies, advertisements and entertainment? These media have frequently

excluded minorities and promoted the "ideal" of healthy, white, blond and slender.

Self-evaluation and Confession

These guidelines require honest self-evaluation. As with any other sin, it is important for each of us to totally confess our participation in prejudicial actions. Then we must be willing to act differently in the future.

The first step in overcoming any sin is confession to God of our conscious and unconscious participation in that sin. Then comes the repentance (forsaking the sin) and the victory. Like many sins, racism may not be overcome instantly. But if we are willing to let God's healing process work, He will be faithful in helping us overcome our sins.

Many Bible-believing, Spirit-filled Christians of every ethnic origin are affected by prejudical thinking and actions. Often by mere neglect well-meaning Christians actually participate in perpetuating racial discrimination and separateness. Instead of trying to see society as Christ would see it, we tend to view the world from our own cultural and racial perspectives.

Christ died for all and He rejected social, racial, economic and sexual distinctions (Gal. 3:28). He saw all as created equally by God with *no distinctions* in the Kingdom of God (Col. 3:11). We are all called to break down man-made distinctions and have our lives and our churches reflect the reality of the Kingdom of God.

Christian activist John Perkins has said that if white people can move beyond their guilt and black people beyond their blame, together we can work to find the necessary change of values, lifestyles and attitudes to experience forgiveness. That forgiveness will transform both races and allow God's Kingdom on earth to become that which would best represent God Himself.

Then we can call to accountability the counselors of this world whose advice is based on racial stereotyping, or the church that sociologically desires to grow, but biblically can't justify separation of the races. When we are able to work seriously in these areas, we will finally become the truly reconciled community Christ called us to be.

Discussion Questions

As the following scenarios are described think about how you have reacted to such situations; how you might react if you encountered them for the first time; how you feel you, as a Christian, *should* respond.

1. You encounter a married couple in a department store. She's white, he's black.

2. An Hispanic person cuts in front of you on the freeway or turnpike, forcing you to quickly apply the brakes.

3. You learn an ethnic couple is moving in next door, and your neighbor across the street complains that the property values will decline.

4. A qualified co-worker is passed over for a promotion in favor of a Vietnamese immigrant equally qualified but who hasn't worked with the company as long.

5. Your son comes home with a new girlfriend. She belongs to your denomination, but her skin is a different color than yours.

6. A fellow worker enjoys telling derogatory ethnic jokes. You laugh, but the the situation makes you uncomfortable.

7. A family of a race other than that of the majority of your church members begins coming to your church. Members of your congregation welcome them but would clearly feel threatened if any more people of another racial group would attend.

CHAPTER 9

The Church and Christians Who "Live Together"

Sunday-morning worship was over. I was standing in the tiled corridor near the entrance to our church, chatting with the few people who still lingered. Suddenly Elaine,* a woman in her mid-twenties and a member of our church, bounced up to me with a look of joy.

"Pastor, guess what!" she blurted out for all to hear. "Keith and I are living together!"

Mouths dropped. I was flabbergasted. The church corridor didn't seem like the place to deal with such an issue, so I urged Elaine to come and discuss her situation with me.

Several months later Elaine and Keith were married. Even though they continued to live together before the wedding, we were able to discuss the biblical view of sex and marriage.

Gregory Stover *is the pastor of Church of the Cross United Methodist in Toledo, Ohio.*

Keith and Elaine are merely one example of a phenomenon which is growing rapidly in American society, a phenomenon which the Church is forced to confront with increasing frequency. In 1970 approximately 523,000 couples in the United States were living together out of wedlock. By 1978 this figure had more than doubled. Recent studies indicate that today perhaps as many as 10 million couples are living together outside the bond of marriage.

My own experience as a pastor has been confirmed by the experiences of other clergy with whom I have discussed this subject. We estimate that one-quarter to one-half of all couples requesting marriage in the Church are already living together.

It might be gratifying if the evangelical wing of the Church could casually glance the other way, giving thanks that such immorality only takes place "out there." But the troublesome fact is, a small, yet increasing number of persons who claim a relationship with Jesus Christ are joining the ranks of those who live together first and marry later.

One such couple came to my office to discuss marriage. The man was quick to relate his experience of new birth which had taken place a few years earlier. Both had been reared with strong Christian values. Yet I learned later in the interview that this couple, in their late forties, had been living together for several months. When I asked how they could claim love for Christ while violating His commandments, the two simply replied that they had no justification and lowered their heads.

How should Christians and the Church as a whole respond to this growing phenomenon? Certainly, if we were to be biblically faithful, the Church should attempt to discourage couples from entering live-in arrangements, while at the same time seeking to minister redemptively to those who do. But how?

Any response will need to take into account some of the *reasons* for the problem.

Perhaps the most obvious reason for the living-together trend is the general moral decline so evident in our society. Sex outside marriage has not only lost its taboo status; it has gained respectability. Nearly every major study of sexual practice verifies that greater numbers of high school and college-age men and women are becoming "sexually active" (a euphemism for *sexually permissive*) at an earlier age.

The television and movie industries have created an aura of acceptability for sexual relationships outside marriage. The National Federation for Decency recently indicated that of all incidents of sexual intercourse portrayed or alluded to on TV, only 15 percent took place within marriage.

Broken Homes

A second reason for the increase in live-in relationships is the lack of stability evident in so many marriages. While America's divorce rate has declined slightly, broken marriages are still exacting a heavy toll in the lives of millions of people.

One teacher told me that, of her 30 elementary pupils, not one is living with both his natural father and mother. The heartache represented in that one classroom is staggering to consider.

Surrounded with marital failure on every side, many couples are saying, "We aren't making any permanent commitments until we have tested our compatibility."

In the logic of the secular world, this apparently makes good sense. Living together will allow adjustments normally made after marriage to be made in a less threatening atmosphere, where commitment is not final or even at issue. If the couple proves incompatible, the error can be rectified before a marriage ensues where the pain and difficulty of separation will be multiplied. So the theory goes. But does it stand the test in real life?

In the February 1984 issue of the *Journal of Marriage and the Family*, Alfred DeMars and Gerald Leslie reported the results of their research with couples who had lived together prior to marriage. DeMars and Leslie hypothesized that couples who lived together before marriage would be better adjusted and more satisfied with marriage.

Questionnaires were sent to 594 couples; 282 wives and 262 husbands responded. The tallies showed that 72 percent of the husbands and 71 percent of the wives had lived together before marriage. DeMars and Leslie discovered:

Couples who lived together before marriage scored *lower* on tests measuring communication in marriage than couples who did not cohabit.

Couples who lived together before marriage also scored *lower* on tests rating marital satisfaction.

Couples who had cohabited before marriage were less prone to stay in a marriage in troubled times than those who had not cohabited before marriage.

Overall, couples who had lived together before marriage had *less satisfying* marriages than those who had not lived together.

These findings seem to illustrate the scriptural teaching that sin exacts a price. Certainly the findings provide hard evidence to dispute the theory that living together before marriage is a good way to test compatibility.

Ministering to the Live-in Generation

Understanding some of the reasons for the living-together phenomenon is important. But a far more pressing issue remains: How do we minister redemptively to today's live-in generation?

First, lay persons can encourage their pastors and youth ministers to teach a truly biblical theology of sex and marriage. Such teaching should be done without embarrassment, shame or fear of the Mrs. Joneses who might huff out of the church protesting, "They never talked about such things in church when I was young."

In all likelihood, Mrs. Jones is right. Sex probably was not mentioned in a worship service when she was young, at least never beyond a few words condemning adultery or pre-marital sex.

However, ours is a vastly changed society. Unfortunately, we no longer have a Christian consensus of values. No longer can we simply declare that God says it's wrong to have a sexual relationship outside the marriage bond and expect people to

The Church and Christians Who "Live Together"

accept it, let alone live it. Our teaching needs to point others toward a truly biblical understanding of our sexuality, the meaning of sexual activity, *why* God has ordained that sex is protected within the confines of the marriage commitment and how the persistent sexual temptations of our society can be overcome.

Second, Christian parents can use real-life situations as "teaching moments" to mold the values and thinking of their children.

Not long ago my wife and I were talking about the recent marriage of a woman, who, in her teen years, bore a child out of wedlock. She raised her son alone, and became a Christian during those years. Now in her forties, she has married a Christian man.

Our six-year-old son asked why she had never been married before. We answered and held our breath anxiously, certain the next question would be, "How did she have a baby if she wasn't married?" Our son did not ask, and we gave thanks!

While we were not yet ready to discuss sex and marriage with our six year old, at some future time, through such a "teaching moment," we will seek to shape his values. We will explain that some people do not treat sex and marriage as God desires. We will tell our son why we hold the values we do. And, perhaps most important, we will emphasize how God transformed this particular woman's life through Christ, despite her previous sin.

Third, when persons who profess Christ as Savior and Lord live together outside marriage, we need to confront them with their sin, gently and lovingly, while looking closely at our own lives lest we fall (Galatians 6:1). Even if our words go unheeded, a faithful witness for Christ will have been established.

Twice in my pastoral experience, my conscience (I trust under the guidance of the Holy Spirit) has compelled me to confront professed believers who, while living together outside of marriage, sought membership in the church. In each incidence I encouraged a change of lifestyles. However, both couples came into church membership after being married.

Fourth, we need to minister to the needs of those who live together, even when their needs and difficulties arise directly from their sinful relationships.

A friend of my wife's and mine became involved in an illicit relationship. It began with occasional sexual encounters and ended in a live-in relationship which our friend hoped would lead to marriage. From time to time my wife and I discussed our friend's situation with her, reminded her of the biblical standard, and encouraged her to re-examine her chosen direction.

When her male friend abruptly ended the relationship in favor of another woman, she was devastated. She went through many of the same emotions and grief reactions that a person experiences in the wake of a divorce or death of a spouse—anger, depression, resentment, guilt, betrayal and loneliness.

Our ministry to such persons should be to the need of the moment. It should be a caring ministry meant to engage the whole person as well as his or her specific sin. Even when we know the hurt is of someone's own making, we must empathize with the hurt—and present Christ, our Forgiver, Comforter and Peace.

Finally, churches can examine, and encourage their pastoral staffs to examine, their wedding policies as they relate to couples who are living together. Does your pastor refuse to marry any who may have cohabited before marriage? Are any conditions placed on the couple living together before they can be married in your church? Does your pastor discuss their situation with them in light of a biblical approach to sex and marriage?

Most people—those living together and not, those who are unchurched and those who are not—still come to the Church for marriage. How your pastor and congregation deal with them provides a powerful statement about the Church's view of sex and marriage, and a poignant testimony for Christ.

A blanket policy of marrying *any* who come may convey the impression that Christ and the Church, His Body on earth, have no standards—that the Church exists for the convenience of the world. A policy of *never* marrying any couple living together may send the message that Christ is graceless, and that the Church exists to judge the world.

The Church and Redemption

In reality, the Church exists to serve her Lord and be His instrument in redeeming the world. Each pastor and congregation could enrich their own understanding of marriage and sex, and their ministry in the midst of a permissive society, by openly dealing with these issues.

Personally, I have become more and more convinced that pastors and congregations need to respond to those who seek marriage, but are already living together, with a word of grace conditioned upon a call to repentance. We need to say, "God loves you, and we too are concerned that you have a satisfying marriage. We would be pleased to assist you in marriage plans. But, in coming to the Church you are implicitly seeking a marriage which is blessed by and honors Christ. From our perspective, when you are married in the Church we are agreeing that yours is a relationship Christ approves. Therefore, before your wedding, we expect you to honestly face the ways you have violated God's design in your relationship and correct them."

To some, I know, this approach will seem unduly harsh. They will be concerned that such a policy will cut off a congregation from ministry to many who are unwilling to change their lifestyles.

Yet, there is room for serious doubt as to whether unquestioningly accommodating to the marriage plans of live-in couples has brought many to Christ or the Church. Instead, when we offer the Church's blessing on marriage at cut-rate prices, we damage the testimony of Christ and do a disservice to the institution of marriage in a society which is moving farther and farther from biblical principles.

The Church does have a ministry, a vital ministry, in the midst of our live-in generation. Our task is to lift up God's design for marriage and sexuality, by word and in the examples of our own lives and marriages. Our task is to respond forthrightly and lovingly to those who deviate from God's design and to point all to the One who gives abundance in singleness and in marriage.

*Names have been changed

Discussion Questions

1. Is the pulpit the proper place to discuss modern sexual lifestyles? Why? Why not?

2. How would you respond if a young adult who respected you came to you with news like Elaine's (page 89)?

3. You are teaching an adult Sunday school class. One of the members questions the Church's position on "trial marriage." Would you be defensive? Taken aback? What would you say?

4. Do you think your pastor should marry two people who have been cohabiting? Why? Why not?

5. If your son or daughter requested a wedding in your church after living with his or her future spouse, would you demand your pastor marry them?

6. If an unmarried couple from your church were living together, do you think the pastor or a layperson should confront them? Why? Why not? If you think they should be confronted, how should it be done?

7. What are some of the consequences of cohabitation, according to the author?

8. How would you respond to the woman whose relationship ended disastrously (page 94)? Did it serve her right? What responsibilities do you, as a Christian have toward her?

9. If a couple asked you *why* they should not live together before marriage, what logical reasons would you give them?

CHAPTER 10

What Can *You* Do About Alcoholism?

The atmosphere at the corporate banquet had storybook grandeur. The evening gowns and tuxedos were elegant. The tables in New York's Waldorf Astoria ballroom were discreetly loaded with all manner of alcoholic beverage that advertisements promote as symbols of distinction.

"I've spoken to the waitress, Frank. She'll bring you a sherry," the vice president told me privately. "We know you prefer not to drink, but you'll appear sociable. The sherry will leave you not looking too 'naked.' " He winked and patted my shoulder in a fatherly fashion and moved on. The gracious host.

Then the waitress arrived—carrying six glasses of sherry! "There is no way I can get around that!" I exclaimed to my dinner

---

Frank Sheldon *is Information Director for the American Alcohol and Drug Information Program of the Michigan Alcohol and Drug Information Foundation and a field speaker for the Michigan Interfaith Council on Alcohol Problems.*

partner, George, whom I'd just met. He was the vice president of a prestigious national corporation.

George motioned toward the engraved place cards. "We apparently were deliberately seated together," he said. "I seldom drink, but I'll help you."

Help he did! The dinner completed, I noticed that my single glass was still unfinished. George, however, had three empties in front of him as he completed the fourth and picked up the final glass to watch the entertainment.

The next morning I joined my hosts for breakfast. "You know, George is an alcoholic," they explained. "He didn't return home last evening. This morning his wife called the office looking for him."

Two weeks later George was located in a flea-bag hotel suffering the ravages of alcoholism.

My hosts spoke of how George had been treated for alcoholism twice at his corporation's expense. His superiors considered him an important asset to the business but warned him the second time, "Stay on the wagon or seek other employment!" Now George had not only lost control over his problem, but he'd also lost his job.

I was stunned. A neophyte in the business world with little knowledge of the part alcohol played in business dealings and of alcoholism, I wished they would have at least warned me. They had a perfect opportunity to use me to support George's need for abstinence. I could have been more firm in my wish to abstain. The most "sociable" act for me would have been to turn the sherry away!

My hosts were decent gentlemen. They cared. But they did not understand the problems of alcohol and their unintentional complicity in George's tragic drama. As for me, rather than helping him, I unwittingly became George's final stumbling block.

Unfortunately there are many "Georges" in our society. According to figures prepared by the National Institute on Alcohol Abuse and Alcoholism (NIAAA):

—34 percent of Americans 14 and older abstain.
—33 percent drink less than once in two weeks.
—23 percent drink 40 percent of all alcohol that is consumed.
—10 percent drink 56 percent of all alcohol that is consumed.

Individuals with alcohol-related diseases are dying at a rate of one every two and one-half minutes! The impact of this national tragedy is multiplied by all the family, business and related connections. The NIAAA estimates the cost of lost productivity, medical care, law enforcement, property damage, hospitalization and lost income at more than $13 million *per hour*. No other natural or man-made tragedy can seem to match it.

Consider some other statistics. Approximately 50,000 young Americans lost their lives in Vietnam. During the war years there were 260,000 fatalities from alcohol-related auto accidents. Another 7,500,000 people were injured in those accidents. The tragedy will continue until someone decides to make a difference. The Body of Christ has that opportunity.

The Body of Christ Cares

Remember Jesus asking us to love God with our whole heart, soul and mind? Remember Paul challenging us to be the Body of Christ? The apostle told the Corinthians that the Body *cares*. He asked the Romans to *think*, while urging them to allow God to remold their minds from within. He explained to the Ephesians how important it is to *respond* to others' needs. Being the Body of Christ, being accountable to each other, being responsible to meet another's needs is a big order. Loving involves every facet of our being. But God has especially designed our bodies to make even loving easier.

In the making of our multi-billion K capacity computer called the central nervous system, God slipped in a micro-chip—the hypothalamus. It controls the heart, lungs, body thermostat, glands, etc., that must function to keep the body alive. The hypothalamus relieves us of wasting time on maintenance matters and frees us to spend more time on creative thinking and problem solving, on loving one another and worshiping God.

Unfortunately the hypothalamus can be handicapped. Dr. Jorge Vales of Baylor University and the Houston Veterans' Administration Hospital has discovered that the hypothalamus is adversely affected by the ingestion of alcohol prior to the time it reaches stability—between the ages of 20 and 22. People who begin drinking before 21 are 300 percent more likely to become alcoholics.

By allowing youngsters to drink, we triple the $13 million hourly cost to society and increase the daily death rate from the abuse of alcohol to more than 1,600. Actuarial tables have indicated that the 14-26 age group is the only group that has not shown an increase in longevity in the last 20 years. Young people are killing themselves with toxic substances which they are ingesting by choice.

Consider one definition of alcohol: "a flammable, toxic compound used in solvents, drugs, cleaning solutions, explosives and in*toxic*ating beverages...harmful, destructive and poisonous." What a shame that so many feel the need to ingest a toxic compound that is also a neuron paralyzer that shuts down our human computer and deadens our senses—even to God.

As a pilot who flew research missions at Edwards Air Force Base in California, the news of the space shuttle Challenger's tragic flight struck me with powerful, empathetic impact! That fateful Tuesday evening we all watched the replays of the explosion, when seven lives were lost. Through the miracle of television we were able to see from the perspective of God, who never misses a single falling sparrow. Are we as sensitive with Him when every two-and-one-half hours seven lives are terminated on American highways in alcohol-related auto crashes?

The frustration I felt over George's problem drew me back to a moment five years earlier when the president of my corporation was about to introduce me to an important customer. I had just been promoted to a significant sales management position—a swift and unexpected promotion—because I was filling the vacancy formed by a resigning alcoholic. The conversation turned to a dinner we'd attended the night before.

"You and your wife barely touched the champagne," the president observed. "Don't you drink?"

"No."

"Why?" he persisted.

With my future with the corporation in possible danger I frantically searched for an appropriate answer. Then he added, "Is it health or religion?"

"Neither," I replied. "I guess that we've never felt the need for it."

"Alcohol is not important to the job, and abstinence is an acceptable lifestyle," he replied. "But if you ever feel the necessity to appear sociable, order sherry. With sherry you'll never get into trouble."

His words later came back to haunt me. Why, I wondered, did alcohol seem to be such an important part of business and social etiquette? I first faced peer pressure as a teenager in the U.S. Army Air Corps during World War II. Getting drunk seemed to be the pastime of most future fighter pilots.

I recall completing a course on engine lubrication, and my fellow cadets asked me again, "Sheldon, why don't you come with us and get drunk? Let's make it a great night on the town!"

The answer seemed logical to me. We were all working hard to become fighter pilots, and we had just learned the importance of filters that kept foreign substances out of the engine. Not one of us scheduled to fly a mission would have thought it a "great night on the town" if someone had dumped a handful of iron filings in the plane's crankcase before takeoff. Why dump a bottle of "iron filings" in your body?

Understanding the Problem

Over the past few years I have realized that my own personal abstinence was not enough. I owe it to others to help them understand the extent of the problems. As a field speaker for the Michigan Interfaith Council on Alcohol Problems, an affiliate of the American Council On Alcohol Problems, I have seen that most people do not realize the extent of the alcohol problem. I inform them and encourage them to seek out their own state's chapter of the ACAP which lobbies in the state capital and initiates awareness programs in schools and churches.

Alcohol abuse kills or injures someone every 33 seconds. We must ask ourselves who will be living a full life tomorrow because of the manner in which we represent Christ.

Many local congregations and national denominations are beginning to become involved in the prevention of alcohol abuse. My denomination, the United Methodist Church, has asked its membership to reconsider abstinence. It's resolutions suggested ways caring Christians could use their time to combat the problems of alcoholism. They offer guidelines people of any faith could apply. In part, the resolutions recommended:

* demonstrating active concern for those with alcohol abuse problems and their families, through members of local congregations.

* demonstrating compassion for the alcoholic through concern by legislative bodies and health care systems.

* making education about alcohol problems and the value of abstinence an integral part of drug education efforts in the church.

* developing responsible attitudes toward alcohol-related problems; care, treatment and rehabilitation of problem drinkers; measures to prevent persons from driving under the influence of alcohol.

* eliminating advertising of alcoholic beverages from television and curbing promotions on the use of alcoholic beverages on college campuses.

* encouraging the health system to accept alcoholism as a medical-social behavioral problem and to treat the alcoholic person with the same consideration given other patients.

*urging the Federal Trade Commission to develop a health hazard warning statement to be affixed to all alcoholic beverages.

*urging the federal government to coordinate its drug and alcohol abuse efforts in treatment and prevention.

* working for raising the minimum legal drinking age to 21 in all states.

In order to consider the issue, Christians need to be informed. We need access to methods of prevention in a culture that legalizes and romanticizes a toxic substance to which so many become addicted. Education and information can lead to prevention, and the Body of Christ can make a difference.

The Apostle Paul said, "God has harmonized the whole body...that the body should work together as whole with all the members in sympathetic relationship with one another. So it happens that if one member suffers all the other members suffer with it..." (1 Cor. 12:24-26, *Phillips*).

The framework for an appropriate lifestyle is available in the teachings of God and Christ. By thinking and caring we can respond intelligently. Then we can be loving supporters of the "Georges" in our lives instead of stumbling blocks.

Discussion Questions

1. Why do you think society for years has been tolerant of alcohol abuse (i.e., drunks on television are "funny," people joking about how drunk someone was at a party)?

2. What effects does alcohol abuse have on the individual, the alcoholic's family, society?

3. Have you known anyone who was injured or killed in an accident where drinking was involved? How did it affect you? How might it affect you?

4. How much do you know about the causes and cures of alcoholism? How can you better inform yourself about the problem?

5. Have you ever felt pressured to drink to be "sociable" by business associates or friends? How did you handle the situation?

6. How would you encourage or advise a Christian who feels pressure to drink?

7. Without "preaching" or exerting undue pressure, how would you counsel a teenager whose peers push him or her to drink to be accepted?

8. Do you know someone who abuses alcohol? What could you do to express compassion and provide help for a person who abuses alcohol? For the family of an alcoholic?

CHAPTER 11

Why Abortion Isn't the Answer

Abortion—right, or wrong?

The question has been tossed around by everyone from the high school debate team to the network news commentator. But for those millions of Americans who face the decision of whether or not to end an unwanted pregnancy, abortion is much more than a topic for discussion. It is literally a matter of life and death. As an obstetrician-gynecologist I had my own personal struggle.

My first encounter with the problem occurred in 1969. I was doing six months of my Mayo Clinic residency at Cook County Hospital in Chicago. I spent six weeks of this time on a ward for infected obstetric patients. My first night on call I naively thought my patients would come from the surgical wards where problems

---

Beverly Ann McMillan, *M.D., is an obstetrician-gynecologist with a private practice in Jackson, Mississippi. She is also involved in public speaking to promote the pro-life position.*

with infection sometimes follow Cesarean deliveries. I soon found out differently.

That night and every night I was on call, 15 to 25 women were admitted to my ward with fevers, bleeding and tender, enlarged uteruses. Many of these women were desperately ill. All night long my intern and I would admit them, start them on intravenous fluids and antibiotics and try to keep them alive until morning. If they survived, we would take them to a treatment room and do a D & C, without anesthesia, to clean out the infected tissue. These women were victims of Chicago's back-alley abortionists.

By the time my six-week stint was finished, I had become an abortionist by conviction. I concluded that if women could be so desperate about an unwanted pregnancy that they were willing to risk a bungled illegal abortion, and if orthodox medicine had the technology to perform safe abortions, then my profession should face its social responsibilities. We should offer such women safe abortions.

When the 1973 Supreme Court decision which legalized abortion, *Roe vs. Wade*, was announced, I welcomed it. I was in private practice in Richmond, Kentucky, by that time. And since abortions were now legal, my partner and I bought a suction machine and began discreetly performing first-trimester abortions in our office.

In the fall of 1974 my family and I moved to Jackson, Mississippi. There I met a group of concerned citizens and clergy who wanted to organize a clinic offering safe abortions on an out-patient basis in the Jackson area. The clinic was about to open, except for one thing. The organizers had not found a physician willing to face the social stigma of being labeled an abortionist. Exercising the courage of my convictions, I volunteered and opened the first legal abortion clinic in the state.

I had come a long way since I attended a Roman Catholic parochial school in my childhood. I had become an agnostic, and I felt I had accomplished all the goals I set out to attain. But even with a successful practice, a stable marriage, three healthy children and most of the material things I wanted, I grew depressed and contemplated suicide.

In desperation I looked for something to read to help me. By chance I happened on *The Power of Positive Thinking* by Dr. Norman Vincent Peale in a local bookstore. At the end of the first chapter Dr. Peale listed 20 things to do to develop a positive attitude. I had no problem with the suggestions except for one which asked me to affirm 10 times daily, "I can do all things through Christ who strengthens me." I felt betrayed and frustrated because I could not repeat the verse, nor could I finish the book.

Finally, after struggling more than a week, I just gave up and said out loud, "I can do all things through Christ who strengthens me." It was in that moment that I submitted my life to Christ.

As I read the Bible over the following months, I felt more and more uncomfortable about performing abortions. I think I was like many Christians in that I felt somehow God did not approve of abortion, but I knew of no hard facts or scriptures to back up my feelings. Nevertheless, I stopped performing abortions personally in 1977, although I continued as medical director of the clinic until 1978.

I began to attend church for the first time in the spring of 1977, and by December of that year I knew God was leading me to be baptized and to identify with His Church. Yet I felt a certain incongruity about a Christian calling herself the medical director of an abortion clinic. So I resigned my position. I've never regretted that decision.

Abortion and the Scriptures

As I grew in my understanding of God and His Word, I discovered *why* I felt uncomfortable with my pro-abortion stand. Since then I have been actively involved in speaking to churches, civic organizations and schools about the abortion situation in the United States. I believe Scripture shows us that God considers unborn human life to be valuable and worthy of our efforts to protect it.

One in every four children conceived is now aborted by legal means, and abortion has become one of the most common surgical procedures in America. Of the 1.5 to 2 million abortions performed annually in the United States, at least 95 percent of them are performed for convenience.

We are told by the pro-abortion movement that a woman has the right to do what she chooses with her own body. It may sound logical, but a woman does not have the right to commit suicide, to appear nude in public places or to willfully spread a communicable disease. The freedom of one person always ends where the freedom of another, in this case the unborn child, begins.

Another argument used to support the idea that abortion should be readily available is that it reduces the number of children abused because they were born as a result of unwanted pregnancies. But child abuse has climbed nearly 400 percent since abortion was legalized. A study of 500 battered children revealed that 90 of them were born to parents who planned the pregnancy.

Those who say legalized abortion keeps poor women from the back-alley abortionists also abuse the facts. Of women seeking abortions, 70 percent are white, 79 percent are unmarried and 75 percent have graduated from either high school or college. Abortion is a middle to upper-middle class problem.

Most abortions are performed to hide or remove the consequences of sexual sin. This matter of personal accountability is one that the Church needs to address today as the fundamental cause of the abortion problem.

The remaining five percent of abortions are performed because of rape, incest, medical illness of the mother and to prevent the birth of "imperfect children." Such cases are more difficult for people who want ethical answers to the abortion problem. But God's Word is not silent in these areas.

I believe the basic principle which underlies God's pro-life position is contained in Genesis 9:6, "Whoever sheds man's blood, by man his blood shall be shed, for in the image of God He made man." Our basic worth stems from the fundamental fact of our creation *in God's image*, and I believe this creation starts from conception.

In Psalm 139, which I like to call the Pregnant Woman's Psalm, God voices His care and concern for the unborn:

"For Thou didst form my inward parts; Thou didst weave me in my mother's womb. I will give thanks to Thee, for I am fearfully and wonderfully made; wonderful are Thy works, and my soul knows it very well. My frame was not hidden from Thee, when I was made in secret, and skillfully wrought in the depths of the earth. Thine eyes have seen my unformed substance; and in Thy book they were all written, the days that were ordained for me, when as yet there was not one of them" (vss. 13- 16).

God cares about human life in the womb and such life has a definite *spiritual* dimension. In the first chapter of Jeremiah, when the prophet receives his call, God says, "Before I formed you in the womb I knew you, and before you were born I consecrated you; I have appointed you a prophet to the nations" (v. 5).

The Incarnation itself reinforces this point. Matthew tells us that Jesus Christ was conceived by the Holy Spirit. "Behold, an angel of the Lord appeared to him in a dream, saying, 'Joseph, son of David, do not be afraid to take Mary as your wife; for that which has been conceived in her is of the Holy Spirit'" (Matthew 1:20).

I remember meditating on this verse and asking myself, "What does conceived by the Holy Spirit mean?" As an obstetrician-gynecologist I certainly knew how every other human being in the world was conceived—a sperm and an egg united and a new cell was formed which contained all that would become the developed human being.

One day it occurred to me that what may have possibly happened in the Incarnation was that the Holy Spirit took on the form of a human sperm and fertilized the egg in Mary's body. From this fertilization the God-man was conceived. If Jesus Christ Himself would sanctify human life by identifying with it from its beginnings at conception, what then should our attitude be toward unborn human life?

Problem Pregnancies

The problems of rape and incest are difficult. Many view allowing such a pregnancy to continue as an unjust form of punishing a woman who has already been abused. However, the circumstance of the conception in such a case does not make the resulting child any less a person made in God's image. The loving thing to do in this circumstance is to offer the woman love and support, both physically and emotionally. She needs help during the difficult pregnancy and while making decisions about whether to keep the child or place it for adoption. Such a solution is not an easy one, but I believe it is the right one.

In the case that a mother's health may be medically worsened by pregnancy, I would state, from a physicians viewpoint, that these cases are very rare. The correct moral decision in this dilemma reflects respect for both the life of the mother and the child, both of whom are created in God's image.

As a pregnancy progresses, a child's chance for survival outside the womb increases. When the mother's condition has reached the point where continuation of the pregnancy is truly dangerous to her health—heart disease or when necessary treatment will be harmful to the baby—then an early delivery should be accomplished. The premature baby should be given every benefit of medical science. In this way respect is shown for both lives.

In the case of so-called "imperfect" children, we are dealing with the ability of medical science to search out and destroy infants who have medical or genetic problems that may leave them mentally retarded or physically handicapped for life. The ethical question of what to do with these imperfect children is certainly addressed in the Bible. After all, we are all God's imperfect children. We are marred by sin. We are not the kind of children God wanted. We have hurt and disappointed Him. In fact, God has a perfect right to destroy us.

But God's response to His imperfect children was to love us, to send His own Son to suffer and die on the cross for us, and through His blood to adopt us back into His family. The Scriptures challenge us to treat our own imperfect children in a similar, loving way.

If abortion on demand were done away with tomorrow, how would I as a Christian confront the problem of women wounded in the illegal abortion mills? I know I would be saddened by their plight, but I would not be outraged. Society must also recognize that it has a fundamental responsibility to protect the life and freedom of those who cannot protect themselves. The entire Christian community must be prepared to respond to the needs of these women with unwanted pregnancies. We must not ostracize them but go to their sides to help them through the physical, emotional, social and financial aspects of their pregnancies. The alternative to abortion is expensive but morally correct.

Statistics show that approximately one in ten American women of reproductive age have had at least one abortion. What of those who must deal with the guilt of abortion? The good news that makes the gospel so relevant is that God forgives. I know from personal experience that the blood of Jesus can cover the sin of abortion.

I once thought abortion was a good thing, the answer to so many social and medical problems. Now I know "there is a way which seems right to a man, but its end is the way of death" (Proverbs 14:12). When I understood the sanctity of unborn human life, I changed my mind about abortion.

Discussion Questions

1. How would you respond intelligently and respectfully to a woman who says:
   a. "I have a right to do what I want with my body"?
   b. "A woman shouldn't be forced to carry out an unwanted pregnancy"?
   c. "What if there's a strong possibilty my child will not be normal"?
   d. "I won't be able to provide a decent standard of living for my child"?

2. Your teenage daughter tearfully tells you she's pregnant and is thinking about an abortion. You are active members of your church, and people in the congregation would be shocked. Would you:
   a. encourage her to marry the baby's father?
   b. encourage her to carry the child to full term and then help her arrange an adoption or help her rear the child?
   c. urge her to have an abortion to allow her to have a fresh start in life?

3. A young woman in your congregation is unmarried and pregnant. She decides she will carry the child to term. Will members of the church:
   a. ask her to leave the church?
   b. tell her they'll pray for her?
   c. visit her and invite her to participate in family events?
   d. help with medical and living expenses?

4. An abortion clinic opens in your community. Would you:
   a. complain to your fellow church members?
   b. work with others on a strategy to close it down, such as organizing picket lines?
   c. work with others to come up with an alternative, such as a counseling center that helps unmarried women emotionally and financially if they decide not to have an abortion?

CHAPTER 12

Divorce, Remarriage and the Bible

The subject of divorce and remarriage has engendered much debate in the Christian community over the past decade. Issues that once seemed cut-and-dried are being challenged. As evangelicals we agree to uphold and abide by scriptural guidelines. So, what does the Bible say about the issue?

Marriage is for life. This is the biblical standard. As early as the second chapter of Genesis we hear God saying, "For this cause a man shall leave his father and his mother, and shall cleave to his wife; and they shall become one flesh" (Genesis 2:24).

Jesus reminds us that marriage makes a couple "no longer two, but one flesh." And He adds, "What therefore God has joined together, let no man separate" (Mark 10:8,9).

J. Harold Greenlee *is a United Methodist minister, a missionary with OMS International and an adjunct professor, University of Texas at Arlington. He earned his Ph.D. from Harvard University and was a Senior Fulbright Fellow, Oxford University.*

God's *perfect* will for humanity has never included divorce. But because of what sin did to human nature, God permitted Moses to allow divorce. Jesus explained it in these terms: "Because of your hardness of heart, Moses permitted you to divorce your wives; but from the beginning it has not been this way" (Matthew 19:8).

Even though divorce is never God's perfect will, there are a few legitimate reasons for ending a marriage.

1. Death. Obviously the death of a spouse is a legitimate ending to a marriage. But because of sin, certain other factors may be the moral equivalent of death. These also provide biblical grounds for ending a marriage.

2. Unfaithfulness. Unrepented immorality kills a marriage just as physical death does. Jesus taught that when a spouse is sexually unfaithful, divorce is permissible (Matthew 19:9).

3. Desertion. Complete and final desertion may also be the moral equivalent of death. Desertion leaves the abandoned partner in the position of widow or widower, deprived of marital rights.

Unfaithfulness and desertion in a marriage are grounds for divorce. But neither factor makes divorce *mandatory*. Through repentance and understanding such marriages can be saved.

As for desertion, it's impossible to set any arbitrary time limit for determining when desertion is final. But an abandoned spouse should give enough time to allow for the possibility of reconciliation.

What does all this mean for the Christian? For one thing, a true follower of Jesus will not seek a divorce except on biblical grounds.

But what if the spouse divorces him or her on non-biblical grounds? Then he or she should be patient, holding the matter before the Lord and looking for the possibility of reconciliation. He or she should continue in this way until the spouse marries someone else or dies; or until it can be seen, with the help of the Holy Spirit, that the desertion is complete and final.

Confusion Over Remarriage

This brings us to the difficult subject of remarriage. There appears to be more confusion among Christians about this issue than about divorce itself.

The problem is illustrated by a man I know who came to Christ after his wife divorced him. The divorce had been caused by *his* unfaithfulness, and his former wife had married again. At that point some other Christians informed him that only two possible conditions could ever give him biblical grounds to marry again: 1) He could marry someone else if his former wife should die. 2) He could marry his former wife again if her present husband should die.

The advice was faulty. My friend's former wife was now "dead" as far as her marriage to him was concerned. And there was no biblical reason why he could not marry another woman, even though he had been the guilty party in his divorce.

In another example, a man deserted his wife for another woman, whom he later married. "As long as you remain married to your second 'wife,' " he was told, "you will be living in adultery." The implication was that his second marriage must be dissolved in order for the adultery to end.

This simply is not true. The adultery consisted of the divorce and the act of the second marriage. But once the marriage was made, even though entering into it was sinful, to dissolve it would only be a further case of adultery.

If such a person wants to get his or her life straightened out with God, the answer is not to destroy another marriage. Instead, he or she should repent of his or her sins, trust Christ as Savior and let God take over his or her life from that point.

God does not demand that a divorced person remain unmarried as a penalty for having become divorced. The biblical interpretations given in some circles almost make divorce the unpardonable sin and prevent divorced people from ever taking positions of leadership in the church.

Some of the confusion about remarriage arises when people treat divorce and remarriage as completely separate issues. In the Gospels, Jesus regularly considers divorce and remarriage *together*. In other words, by the way Jesus treats these issues, He implies that biblical grounds for divorce are also biblical grounds for remarriage.

Someone may offer Paul's statement in I Corinthians 7:10-11 as evidence that the Bible does separate the issues of divorce and remarriage. In this passage Paul counsels wives not to leave their husbands. Then, he adds, "If she does leave, let her remain unmarried, or else be reconciled to her husband" (v. 11).

We must remember though that Paul does not use the word for "divorce" here. He uses the word for "separate." And what if we could include the idea of divorce in this passage? Even then, Paul gives no indication that the wife has biblical grounds for divorce. If not, she shouldn't remarry, but rather she should seek a reconciliation. This wouldn't necessarily apply, though, if she had biblical grounds for divorce.

Paul's statement here does not contradict the principle implied by Jesus: that grounds for divorce are also grounds for remarriage. In fact, nowhere does the New Testament teach that divorce is legitimate in cases where remarriage is not permitted.

Divorce and Adultery

Further, the biblical view is that the act of illegitimate divorce itself constitutes adultery, as well as marriage to another person afterward. Remember Jesus' discussion of divorce in Mark 10? "What therefore God has joined together, let no man separate" (vss. 8-9). The clear implication is that breaking the "one flesh" union is sinful and adulterous.

Matthew 5:32 supports this view, although this passage has been almost universally misinterpreted. Most Bible translations are similar to the New American Standard: "But I say to you that everyone who divorces his wife, except for the cause of unchastity, makes her commit adultery; and whoever marries a divorced woman commits adultery."

Divorce, Remarriage and the Bible

But Bible translator Ray Elliott points out that the verb translated "makes (her) commit adultery" is not in the active voice as it is rendered here. It is rather in the passive voice. The phrase should literally read, "causes her to be committed adultery against."

Proper attention to this verb shows that Jesus is literally saying, "Whoever divorces his wife, except for immorality causes her to be the victim of his adultery in divorcing her...." Divorce is adultery here.

We must keep in mind that no single New Testament passage gives the complete picture concerning divorce. For example, none of the four Gospel passages states that a *woman* may divorce her husband if he is unfaithful. But we may assume that this is permitted for a wife as well as for a husband.

Also, Matthew 5:32 and Luke 16:18 state that a man who marries a divorced woman commits adultery. But in view of the larger picture we must assume that this does not apply if the woman has divorced her husband on biblical grounds, or if her former husband has died or remarried.

In I Corinthians 7, Paul states that a wife should not separate from her husband, but if she does, she should remain unmarried or be reconciled to her husband. He adds that this principle applies to husbands as well (vss. 10,11).

Then in verse 15 Paul states that if an unbelieving husband or wife chooses to leave a Christian spouse, "...let him leave; the brother or sister is not under bondage in such cases...." Paul adds no admonition to remain unmarried. So the Christian is evidently free to remarry if it becomes clear that the unbelieving spouse has deserted in a final sense.

A Summary

To summarize the points made about divorce and remarriage:
* Divorce is contrary to God's plan for mankind.
* The biblical grounds for divorce are unfaithfulness or desertion by a non-Christian partner. Some evangelicals

(including me) believe that final desertion, even by a Christian, constitutes death to the marriage.

* If a Christian becomes involved in a non-biblical divorce or separation, he or she should try for reconciliation. But if one of the partners marries someone else or dies, no possibility for reconciliation remains. In that case the other partner is free to remarry, no matter who was the guilty party. In other words, the remarriage of one divorced spouse is the equivalent of death, so far as the former marriage is concerned.

Beyond all the considerations which we have discussed, we must never lose sight of the fact that God accepts us as we are and where we are. If a non-Christian who has been divorced on non-biblical grounds and has remarried comes to God in repentance and faith in Christ, God forgives him or her for the sin of divorce just as for all other sins.

The same is true if a Christian becomes involved in divorce and remarriage on non-biblical grounds. If the individual truly repents, God forgives him or her.

One final word should be said. The New Testament gives guiding principles which are permanent and authoritative. But they are not detailed answers for each specific situation. In life situations, more than one biblical principle may apply and all must be considered together.

This is true in regard to divorce and remarriage. For example, suppose a husband is not guilty of sexual unfaithfulness, but treats his wife and children with such cruelty that their emotions and even their lives may be in danger. The mother's God-given responsibility for herself and her children might dictate, under the guidance of the Holy Spirit, separation or even divorce.

This is not to suggest a weakening of God's standard concerning divorce. Rather it points out that the Bible's teaching on divorce and remarriage must, in actual situations, be considered together with any other of God's laws and principles which apply. In decisions about divorce and remarriage, as in all of life, Christians are called to walk in the light of biblical principles and with the guidance of the Holy Spirit.

Discussion Questions

1. Read Matthew 5:32, Luke 16:18, Mark 10:11-12 and 1 Corinthians 7:10-15. What are grounds for divorce? Under what conditions may a person remarry?

2. In light of this study, what questions would you ask a Christian who is considering divorce?

3. What questions would you ask a divorced person considering remarriage?

4. How would you counsel a person who has obtained a divorce for unbiblical reasons, has remarried and is now experiencing guilt over the situation?

5. How would you counsel the victim of an unbiblical divorce if the guilty spouse *has not* remarried? If the spouse *has* remarried?

6. By agreeing there are biblical grounds for divorce, should you encourage an offended spouse to sue for divorce? Why? Why not?

7. Do you feel your church has a balanced view of divorce and remarriage, i.e., stressing the importance of marriage as a permanent commitment without treating divorce as an unpardonable sin? What can you do to bring about balance?

CHAPTER 13

Morality Matters in Money Management

If you were to mention morality and personal finances in the same breath, most people would give you a puzzled look. The two seem to be unrelated. But, if you asked, "What does money have to do with morality?" Most would say, "Plenty!" Perhaps "money" brings to mind the lifestyles and spending habits of the rich and famous whose abundant cash allows them to indulge in every whim. But when we hear "personal finances" we think of our own limited, perhaps even meager, resources.

Now if you and I are average Americans, we must honestly admit that the amount of legal tender passing through our hands in a lifetime is staggering in comparison to the finances of our

Donald L. Shell *was formerly manager of Advanced Engineering for General Electric and now lives in Lake Junaluska, North Carolina. He holds an M.S. in applied science and a Ph.D. in mathematics from the University of Cincinnati.*

grandparents, not to mention most of the rest of the world. Because we do have so much, it is our moral responsibility to handle it wisely.

For much of my life this concern was largely neglected. For example, I would occasionally take my family on a vacation to some interesting part of the country. We frequently "economized" by not visiting attractions along the way if they required entrance fees. Because of this, we missed out on many opportunities for fun, relaxation and growth. I now see this as a false economy since most of the expense involved travel, meals and lodging. The small cost of entrance fees would have greatly increased the pleasure and value of those trips.

In effect, we wasted resources on those trips because we weren't thinking clearly. We let most of our spending just happen rather than deliberately planning our lifestyle and spending patterns. As a result, our financial philosophy developed haphazardly rather than according to a thoughtful plan.

In evaluating spending habits, the first thing that comes to mind is giving. The tithe is the standard mentioned in the Scriptures and I believe it is the minimum norm for Christians. All tithing Christians I've known seem to be blessed with real joy in giving. Some Christians have also received the spiritual gift of giving. I've heard of people who have given away as much as 90 percent of their income. Often they have been blessed with abundant resources to give away.

Recently a young couple of my acquaintance began tithing, although their budget barely seemed to stretch far enough to cover the family's needs. They made their decision after observing another tithing family that seemed to be blessed in their giving. A few days after making that decision, the young mother stumbled over some unbelievable bargains in school clothing for the children. Several similar events happened in succession. The couple reported that since beginning to tithe their income seemed to cover their needs better than it had before. What they were giving away did not subtract from what they needed.

Part of being a good steward also requires that we give responsibly. In recent years scandals involving television ministries should have made us aware of the need to know how our gifts are being used. That applies to the United Way, the local church, a faith mission, a university scholarship or a special denominational fund-raising project. I did not always make the effort to obtain such information and some of my donations have supported causes I didn't really believe in and which probably did not please God. One time I responded to an attractive cause without inquiring about it. Later I learned that about 90 percent of the gifts were used to pay the collection agency and only 10 percent ever went to that attractive cause. What a disappointment!

Your Daily Spending

The most common acting out of our philosophy is our daily spending. We generally spend most of our money on ourselves, our families and our friends. But the question is, are we spending responsibly or are we being inattentive in our habits?

It is interesting to watch the way people shop in supermarkets. I've seen some check out with a large supply of beer, soft drinks, TV dinners, snack foods and cigarettes. I've watched others purchase fruit, vegetables, meat, milk and other staples. The contrast in priorities is remarkable.

Scripture says that Christians' bodies are dwelling places of the Holy Spirit. That should motivate us to take good care of our bodies and therefore avoid buying things that would weaken and destroy our bodies.

The same principle would apply to boycotting the products of companies that sponsor offensive television programming, pollute the environment or endanger the health and well-being of people. Through the National Federation for Decency I have become aware that one national hotel chain has made pornographic movies available to their guests. So, my wife and I no longer stay in those particular hotels when we travel.

Our spending philosophy is also connected to our tastes in entertainment, clothing, transportation and housing. One person may buy stereo equipment instead of supplementing his wardrobe. Someone else drives an old car so he or she can afford a nice apartment. Other people place high priorities on entertainment, dining out, health club memberships, hobbies, vacations, etc. None of these things are necessarily bad in themselves. But a person knows better how to spend his or her money after figuring out what is most important.

Another thing to think about is how we save and invest. Some people make no attempt to save. We think of them as spendthrift, careless, thoughtless and irresponsible. Some people do without to save every possible penny. We think of them as hoarding, penny-pinching, selfish and miserly. Either extreme is undesirable.

Saving is clearly a matter of choice. By saving we choose to be prepared for an unexpected emergency. If, for instance, the car breaks down we won't be marooned indefinitely if we have emergency savings to fall back on. By saving we also choose to forego some pleasure or convenience now so we can afford a more desirable (and probably more expensive) thing later, such as a special trip or a new car.

Another idea to consider is that by saving we prepare for our own future care when we retire and can no longer produce a regular income. On a larger scale, savings are the capital that makes our economy run well.

In the last few years much has been said about how to invest and disinvest with moral responsibility. There are terrible dilemmas involved, and we must use good judgment. For example, if I own stock in a company I now deem to be immoral, can I in good conscience sell it to someone else? Again, information is the key in making investments wisely and responsibly.

One more area to be addressed is credit. Credit card debt has become a major problem in this country, a result of the "buy now, pay later" philosophy. Instead of saving for major purchases, we obtain what we want now instead of waiting until we can afford the items. Credit cards are not bad in themselves—they can be helpful when check cashing is difficult and in times of emergency.

They generally don't cause you trouble either if you pay the balance every month, but if you don't, the interest charges add up.

One thing we can do to avoid going into unnecessary debt is to simply live within our means. A Charles Dickens character said, "Earn 20 shillings, spend 19, that's heaven. Earn 20 shillings, spend 21, that's hell." The comment seems comically simple, but I knew a family a few years ago that inherited a home debt free. Seven years later they owed $42,000 on a home mortgage and needed to borrow more. Why? They were spending $500 more per month than their income. They clearly needed a change in lifestyle to become financially and morally responsible.

As we reflect on our giving, spending and saving, we see that handling personal finances does involve moral questions. But how do we make the many decisions involved without agonizing over every penny? As in all other areas of life, our lifestyles and values dictate most of our decisions in advance. Throughout life, whether we realize it or not, we are establishing a pattern of living, a philosophy of giving, spending and saving. In the process, we are establishing guidelines for ourselves which help us decide quickly how we respond to financial situations. As a result, we automatically send a check to some charities who request money and just as firmly turn down others. Similarly we automatically buy certain kinds of food and clothing and ignore others. All of these decisions are governed by our personal financial patterns and lifestyles.

Evaluating Your Finances

Therefore, it is important to stop and evaluate patterns of spending and to readjust our philosophies of finances where it does not conform to what we feel is pleasing to God. That may sound like an imposing task, but I have some suggestions:

1. Decide that your personal finances *do* involve moral choices.

2. Examine your present lifestyle with this decision in mind. One thing you might find helpful would be to write down

everything you spend for one month. You might be amazed at where the money goes and it will give you a good idea of what has been important to you.

3. Decide to give a definite percentage of your income before taxes. I suggest 10 percent as a goal. Some people give more, some less. Still, your Christian lifestyle will require a disciplined giving.

4. Become informed about your church and other groups to which you give. Give to those causes and organizations that are doing the things you really believe in. Look beyond the labels. Not every cause with a proper label will fit with your philosophy and lifestyle. Even some causes promoted by your church may prove lacking when you examine them closely.

5. Look at your savings and investments. Are they growing sensibly? Will they contribute to your future well-being? Do they support the kind of institutions that represent good in the world?

6. Evaluate your spending patterns, decide which ones should be changed and make those changes. For example, a couple decides their children do not read enough. So they cut $10 per month from their video rental budget to buy books. Another person decides he's spending too much money on fast food. He decides to stay away from the hamburger stand for a week in favor of having dinner in a nicer restaurant once a week.

7. Except in emergencies, decide you will not use your credit cards unless you can pay for the item when the monthly bill comes.

8. Review your financial situation, your philosophy and the changes you've made next year.

With this kind of deliberate approach to your personal financial lifestyle, you can be confident that you are being a good steward of your resources.

Discussion Questions

1. In what ways can you say that a person's spending habits are a reflection of his or her lifestyle?

2. What are your spending priorities beyond basic necessities (food, housing, clothing and medical expenses)?

3. Think about the number of credit cards in your wallet? How often do you use them? How many times do you retain a balance from month to month?

4. How often do you buy things with a credit card that you might not ordinarily have purchased if you would have had to pay cash?

5. Do you feel budgets are restrictive or helpful? Why?

6. Think of the non-profit Christian organizations to which you give and your church's programs. What do you know about how the money is spent?

7. Think about the amount of your income you give to your local church and to mission and para-church organizations. Do you feel you are giving enough?

8. Why do you think people resist giving?

9. Evaluate your debts. Do some of them exist because your tastes are too expensive for your income? How can you make wiser choices in the future?